RACE
to OBLIVION:

*A Participant's View
of the Arms Race*

HERBERT YORK

SIMON AND SCHUSTER · NEW YORK

SBN 671-20610-9
Library of Congress Catalog Card Number: 74-125601
Designed by Edith Fowler
Manufactured in the United States of America

CONTENTS

Introduction

PROLOGUE:
EISENHOWER'S
OTHER WARNING

President Eisenhower's farewell address is justly famed for the twin warnings it left with the American people. The first of these concerned the possibility of "the acquisition of unwarranted influence, whether sought or unsought, by the military-industrial complex." Arms-control advocates sometimes use it as if it came from a sacred litany. Military-power advocates and arms developers feel compelled to explain it away by emphasizing other passages in the same speech. Scholars and politicians contend it is incomplete, and speak of the military-industrial-X complex, where X can stand for such other institutions as labor unions or universities or Congressional committees or combinations of them.

The other warning which directly followed the first—and which he placed on the same footing—is much less widely known, seldom quoted, and often poorly understood. After noting that research played an increasingly crucial role in our society and that the ways in which it was conducted had changed radically in recent years, Eisenhower said, *Yet in holding scientific research and discovery in respect, as we should, we must also be alert to the equal and opposite danger that public policy could itself become the captive of a scientific-technological elite.*

Because this warning is the more subtle, it is the more difficult to interpret; for the same reason it is the more important.

President Nixon and high defense officials have suggested that the opposition by some scientists to the deployment of ABM missiles was what President Eisenhower had in mind. The physicists' vote against the ABM, taken after the spring 1969 meeting of the American Physical Society, was described as an example of an attempt by this elite to exercise illicit power. However, I think that what President Eisenhower really did have in mind is something very different from and much more significant than the type of thing suggested by these recent interpretations.

I worked fairly closely with Dwight D. Eisenhower during the last three years of his Presidency, first as a member of the Science Advisory Committee he set up immediately after Sputnik under the chairmanship of James R. Killian, Jr., and second as the first Director of Defense Research and Engineering, a new position created by the Defense Reorganization Act of 1958. In these jobs, I was directly concerned with precisely those scientific and technological programs in which the President himself was most involved, and I think, therefore, I have a good feeling for the context in which his thinking on the subject took place.

It also happened that after leaving the Presidency Eisenhower spent his winters in Palm Desert, California, a town less than one hundred miles from my home, and I called on him there on several occasions to pay my respects. Much of our conversation on those visits was devoted to the two warnings. He told me quite specifically that he had just two purposes in mind in making his farewell address. One was to say goodbye to the American people, whom he deeply loved. The other was to bring before the people precisely these warnings. The rest of the speech, he said, perhaps with some exaggeration, was there simply to fill it out and make the whole thing the appropriate length for a farewell address. I asked him to explain more fully what he meant by the warnings, but he declined to do so, saying he didn't mean anything more detailed than what he had said at the time. I knew him well enough to understand what he meant: these warnings were not the result of a careful, methodical analysis; rather, they were the product of a remarkable intuition whose power has generally been underestimated.

What, then, was the context of these remarks? What annoyed and irritated him? Just whom are we to be wary of?

The context spanned the forty months from the launching of Sputnik to the end of his administration. The people who irritated him were the hard-sell technologists who tried to exploit Sputnik and the missile-gap psychosis it engendered. We were to be wary of accepting their claims, believing their analyses, and buying their wares.

The hard-sell technologists and their sycophants invented the term "missile gap," and they embellished that simple phrase with ornate horror stories about imminent threats to our very existence as a nation. They then promptly offered a thousand and one technical delights for remedying the situation. Most were expensive, most were complicated and baroque, and most were loaded more with engineering virtuosity than with good sense. Anyone who did not immediately agree with their assessments of the situation and who failed to recognize the necessity of proceeding forthwith on the development and production of their solutions was said to be unable to understand the situation, technically backward, and trying to put the budget ahead of survival.

The claims of such people that they could solve the problem if only someone would unleash them carried a lot of weight with the public and with some segments of the Congress and the press. Other scientists and technologists had performed seeming miracles in the recent past, and it was not unnatural to suppose that they could do it again. It seemed that radar had saved Britain, that the A-bomb had ended the war, and that the H-bomb had come along in the nick of time to save us from the Russian A-bomb. On the home front, antibiotics had saved our children from the scourges of earlier times, machines had uplifted us from drudgery, airplanes and electronics could carry us and our words great distances in short times. Scientists and technologists had acquired the reputation of being magicians who were privy to some special source of information and wisdom out of reach of the rest of mankind. A large part of the public was therefore more than ready to accept the hard-sell technologist's view of the world and to urge that the government support him in the manner to which he wanted to become accustomed. It seemed as if the pursuit of expensive and complicated technology as an end in itself might very well become an accepted part of America's way of life.

But it was not only the general public that believed the technologists understood something the rest of the world could not. Many of the technologists themselves believed that only they understood the problem. As a consequence, many of them believed it was their patriotic duty to save the rest of us whether or not we wanted them to. They looked at what the Soviets had done. They used their own narrow way of viewing things to figure out what the Russians ought to have done next. They decided then that since the Russians were rational (about these things anyway), what they ought to have done next was what they must now be doing, and they then determined to save us from the consequences of this next Russian technological threat. The Eisenhower Administration was able to deal successfully and sensibly with most of the resulting rush of wild ideas, phony intelligence, and hard sell. But some of these ideas did get through, at least for a while. Beyond that, dealing with self-righteous extremists who have all the answers —and there were many among the aerospace scientists and technologists at the time—is always annoying and irritating.

As we now know, the Byzantine technological ideas urged on us in those years were in fact a portent of things to come.

Weapons systems have become still more complex in the years since Eisenhower's farewell address. And this complexity is creating new and serious problems of the general kind that Eisenhower warned us about. Worse, this complexity involves not only the inner workings of any device but its use and application as well. By 1969, on the problem of what to do about defending our land-based missiles, one expert felt obliged to say, "The judgment about the best means should be based on a complex of factors that can scarcely be grasped whole by a full-time Secretary of Defense. That a committee of the Congress could meaningfully penetrate such a judgment seems to be most unlikely." I do not believe that this statement was true insofar as the judgment concerning the specific question at issue was concerned, but Donald Brennan, who made the statement, is a long-time serious student of military technology and we must therefore take it as at least a warning of what may become true. And when such a statement can be correctly made about a large issue like protecting land-based missiles, then indeed "public policy" will have been, as Eisenhower warned, "captured by a scientific-technological elite." To allow this to happen would be to accept an absurdity: the transfer of control over our destinies from ourselves and the statesmen and politicians we select into the eager hands of strategic analysts, technologists, and other experts.

We will see in this book how the over-all complexity of systems is already leading us to a situation in which the response to a hypothetical future attack will be so complicated and the time in which to decide what to do will be so short that it will be necessary to turn to automatic computing machines for the purpose. If we continue with the present style of technological approach to defense problems, the inclusion of human beings in the decision-making loop will seriously degrade the performance of the system. Thus, here too the power to make life-and-death decisions is passing from the hands of statesmen and politicians to lower-level officers and ultimately to computing machines and the technicians who program them. This trend too, if allowed to continue, will result in the capture of public policy by a scientific-technological elite. Eisenhower's warnings, while based largely on intuition, have pointed up a very real and extremely serious problem.

1

THE ARMS RACE AND I

Germany invaded Poland and started World War II just two weeks before I entered the University of Rochester in September, 1939. Ever since then, my professional life has been completely dominated by the nuclear-arms race.

During my sophomore and junior years my physics professors, including Lee DuBridge and Victor Weisskopf, began to disappear one by one into secret war laboratories. After my own accelerated graduation in May, 1943, I too left for the University of California Radiation Laboratory in Berkeley, where we were engaged in the separation of uranium isotopes. The director of the laboratory was Ernest O. Lawrence, and my immediate boss was Frank Oppenheimer. Frank's older brother, J. Robert Oppenheimer, was at that time establishing a laboratory at Los Alamos, New Mexico, where the isotopes we were separating would, two years later, be fabricated into history's first atomic weapon.

After spending the rest of 1943 at the laboratory in Berkeley, I went with a number of others to Oak Ridge, Tennessee, where we assisted in starting up the great Y-12 manufacturing plant, whose processing machinery was a simple direct multiplication of the isotope separation devices we had been working on in California. Finally, on August 6, 1945, the uranium isotopes we had separated with a late assist from the K-25 plant also located at Oak Ridge were detonated over Hiroshima, in history's first military use of nuclear explosives. On August 9, another A-bomb, made from a different nuclear explosive (plutonium), produced by an entirely different process, was exploded over Nagasaki.

The very next day the Emperor of Japan announced to the world his desire to surrender. We had every reason then to believe that our bombs had caused him to do so.

A few weeks after, my father, who was a Railway Express messenger, came down to Oak Ridge on his pass to visit me. As we sat on a hill overlooking the great Oak Ridge isotope-separation plant, I explained to him how we had finally succeeded in making war so terrible that it could not happen again. I really believed it. I was just twenty-three and I did not yet know that the same thing had been said many times before. I think I would have believed it anyway, if only because this latest step up in the horror of war was such a huge one. It was only much later, after still further enormous increases in the potential destructiveness of war, that I came to realize that we had made perhaps no change at all in the probability of war.

I returned to Berkeley in 1945 as a student and embarked on a career in pure science, or so I thought at the time. Four years later, in June, 1949, I received my Ph.D. Two months after that the Russians exploded their first atomic bomb. This explosion, which happened much sooner than most experts had believed possible, was followed only ten months later, in June, 1950, by the sudden outbreak of the Korean War. As with many other Americans, my life was radically changed again by these two events and by my view of them. Stalin was very much alive, the Sino–Soviet alliance had just been forged, and the future looked gloomy once again.

Edward Teller began to promote the idea that the United States, in response to the new situation, should initiate a top-priority program to develop a hydrogen bomb. He, with others at the Los Alamos Scientific Laboratory, designed an experimental device which they believed could establish the conditions necessary to bring about the nuclear ignition of the appropriate forms or isotopes of hydrogen. Hugh Bradner and I joined a number of others in establishing at Berkeley a group that later set up at Eniwetok an experimental apparatus to study the environmental conditions within which this hydrogen reaction was supposed to take place. In May, 1951, in Operation Greenhouse at Eniwetok, this hydrogen burn, or fusion, did come about more or less as expected, and our experiment helped to confirm the possibility of turning it into a weapon.

Shortly after, I was appointed an assistant professor of physics at the University of California, Berkeley, and the next fall I began once again, I thought, a research and teaching career. I was just getting settled into that job when Ernest Lawrence asked me to take the lead in establishing a branch of the Radiation Laboratory to undertake research and development in the fields of nuclear explosives and controlled fusion reactions. Edward Teller, Harold Brown, John S. Foster, Jr., and I, along with two hundred others altogether, opened shop in September, 1952, in a grape-growing valley at Livermore, California. As was his own special style, Lawrence at first simply told me to "run the place." Later, after we had been going for a little more than a year, he told me to "start calling yourself the director," and I did. Our first attempts to design nuclear explosives worked out poorly. The first two shots at the Nevada test site in the spring of 1953 gave less than the expected explosive yields. In the following year, at Bikini, our first attempt produced an outright fizzle, and we then canceled what would have been our second shot in that test series after painfully deducing that it would turn out the same way. Even so, we all kept trying, and eventually the Livermore Laboratory, now known as the Lawrence Radiation Laboratory/Livermore, succeeded in developing its share of America's nuclear weapons.

Toward the end of my tenure at Livermore, we began to get

involved in a small way with the group President Eisenhower had set up under Harold Stassen for the purpose of trying to find and promote steps leading to arms control and disarmament. It was at that time that I first came to realize that there was another side to the arms race and that there might really be some other more promising and less dangerous road to national security. I came to this realization later than some older and more perceptive scientists, but, even so, earlier than many others.

As director of the Livermore Laboratory, I was invited in 1954 by John von Neumann to join a special committee which he chaired. This committee had as its purposes, first, reviewing various proposals for the development of huge rockets capable of delivering nuclear warheads with high accuracy a quarter of the way around the world, and, second, advising the Air Force (and later the Secretary of Defense) as to what should be done to overcome the Soviets' earlier start in this new field of weaponry. (By 1953 our intelligence confirmed that the Soviet Union, building on the earlier programs of the Germans in World War II, was engaged in a major effort to develop long-range rockets capable of delivering nuclear warheads.)

The Von Neumann Committee was remarkable in style as well as output. In its earliest meetings, the committee worked directly and intimately with Assistant Secretary of Defense Donald Quarles, Air Force Brigadier General Bernard A. Schriever, and Trevor Gardner, Special Assistant to the Secretary of the Air Force for Research and Development. It was instrumental in establishing the Ramo-Wooldridge Corporation in its role of what is now called "general systems engineering and technical direction" (GSETD) of all Air Force long-range-missile programs. It also established the basic design parameters for all the large rockets that the United States developed in the ensuing years. Other members of this remarkable committee included Charles A. Lindbergh and Clark B.

Millikan—who became chairman after the untimely death of Von Neumann—as well as George B. Kistiakowsky and Jerome B. Wiesner, both of whom later became Special Assistants for Science and Technology to Presidents of the United States.

On October 4, 1957, the Soviets launched Sputnik, the first artificial earth satellite, and my professional life underwent another sudden and drastic change. In response to this and to other Soviet space achievements that quickly followed, President Eisenhower appointed James R. Killian, Jr., then president of the Massachusetts Institute of Technology, to be his Special Assistant for Science and Technology and to establish and chair the President's Science Advisory Committee. Killian and I had met previously in connection with the work of the Gaither panel, and I was most fortunate to be among those he invited to join the committee. I took a temporary leave (I thought) from my post as director of the Livermore Laboratory, and began in December, 1957, to spend full time working with the committee (called PSAC, pronounced pea'–sack) in the White House annex. I thus had a front seat from which to watch our efforts to "do something" about the Soviets' "firsts," and I was able to participate in the making of many of the decisions involved. PSAC reaffirmed some of the old priorities and established some new ones in the United States' space and missile programs. PSAC encouraged and then endorsed the efforts of the Department of Defense to get its house in order in this area, and was the most important factor in transforming NACA (the National Advisory Committee for Aeronautics, an organization conducting research in aeronautics) into NASA (the National Aeronautics and Space Administration, the organization responsible for all the non-military aspects of the United States' space program). But, in addition, PSAC even then found time to devote much of its attention to the problem of containing the arms race. In general PSAC developed ideas of how best to organize for arms control; in particular, it did the lion's share of the work involved in promoting the nuclear-test moratorium of 1958. I did not have a major role in that part of PSAC's work at the time, but I followed it closely and was very much impressed by it. What I learned there greatly influenced my own direct activities in arms control and disarmament, which began somewhat later.

I never did go back to Livermore. In the spring of 1958 I was invited by Secretary of Defense Neil H. McElroy to become the chief scientist of the Advanced Research Projects Agency. ARPA, as the agency is usually called, was one of the Department of Defense's responses to the shock of the series of Soviet firsts in space. Each of the three military services was determined to take advantage of the frantic Congressional and public reaction to the spectacular Soviet successes, and each began to lay its own claims to the various new roles and missions it foresaw in this new environment.

The Navy was already the agent for the Vanguard program that was to have launched America's first satellite; the Air Force then already had the responsibility and the money for the development of the largest of the long-range rockets; the Army had Wernher von Braun. ARPA, therefore, was established in large part to try to bring this very confusing and politically explosive situation under control. Roy W. Johnson, a General Electric executive, was named Director of the new agency, Rear Admiral John Clark was named its Deputy Director, and I became its Chief Scientist. We opened for business in late February, 1958, and we did help to produce some order in the space and missile efforts of the Department of Defense.

In December, 1958, I was appointed the first Director of Defense Research and Engineering by President Eisenhower, on nomination by Secretary McElroy and with the advice and consent of the Senate. As set out in the Defense Reorganization Act of 1958 (another American response to Sputnik), the DDRE (as the incumbent of the position is labeled) had authority over all research, development, tests, and evaluation programs of the Department of Defense and its component parts. In addition, he had the responsibility to advise the Secretary of Defense with regard to certain other matters, including the deployment of advanced types of weapons systems. I continued to serve as the DDRE under Secretary Thomas S. Gates, and briefly also under Secretary Robert S. McNamara after being reappointed by President Kennedy. It was an exceptionally interesting time to be in a job of that sort; the general form of nearly all of our present missile and space programs was jelled at that time. It was the time when the Von Braun group was transferred from the Army to NASA and when the responsibility for the very large rockets was also transferred from ARPA to NASA. It was also the time of the first rejection of the proposal to deploy an ABM (antiballistic-missile) system, and it was the time of the U-2. It was during my tenure in that job as scientific administrator of the United States side of the arms race that I formed the views I still hold about the futility of the race and the absolute need to find some alternative course.

In January, 1961, I had the opportunity to discuss these matters with John J. McCloy, who was President-elect Kennedy's personal and principal adviser on matters of arms control and disarmament. I communicated to Mr. McCloy the substance of what I stated publicly before the Senate Foreign Relations Committee in 1963:

> Ever since shortly after World War II, the military power of the United States has been steadily increasing; over the same period the national security of the United States has been rapidly and inexorably diminishing. . . . It is my view that the problem posed to both sides by this dilemma of steadily increasing military power and steadily decreasing national security has no technical solution. If we continue to

look for solutions in the area of military science and technology only, the result will be a steady and inexorable worsening of this situation. I am optimistic that there is a solution to this dilemma; I am pessimistic only insofar as I believe there is absolutely no solution to be found within the areas of science and technology.

After the inauguration of President Kennedy, McCloy became responsible for developing and promoting the legislation which led to establishment of the United States Arms Control and Disarmament Agency. When the agency was formed, he became Chairman of its General Advisory Committee, and I became one of the committee members.

Some months after Robert S. McNamara became Secretary of Defense I resigned as DDRE so that I could return, as I had long been planning, to the University of California. At his request, I gave Secretary McNamara a list of thirteen names of persons who could, I believed, easily replace me. (I consulted Killian, Kistiakowsky, Wiesner, Glenn T. Seaborg and many others in making up my list.) The name McNamara picked was that of my good friend Harold Brown, who at the time was director of the Livermore Laboratory, as I had been earlier. When Brown later became Secretary of the Air Force, he was in turn succeeded as DDRE by another mutual friend, John S. Foster, Jr., who had followed Brown as director of the Livermore Laboratory.

After returning to the University of California, first as chancellor of the San Diego campus and later as professor of physics, I kept posted on the arms race and the efforts to bring it under control, through continuing service as a member of the General Advisory Committee of the Arms Control and Disarmament Agency (from 1963 to 1969), as a member of the President's Science Advisory Committee for a second term (1964–68), and also as a trustee of two nonprofit corporations: the Aerospace Corporation (the organization now charged with doing general systems engineering and technical direction for most of the Air Force's space and missile programs) and the Institute for Defense Analyses (which, among other things, performs analyses and makes studies of weapons systems for the Joint Chiefs of Staff, the Secretary of Defense, and other high government officials).

After finishing my second term on PSAC, I began my fourth attempt to establish a serious career in basic science, this time by teaching physics and doing a modest amount of laboratory work. Fifteen months later, in the spring of 1969, when the matter of the deployment of the ABM suddenly broke from behind the curtain of secrecy to become a public issue, I welcomed the opportunity to testify before the Congress on three occasions in opposition to the deployment of what President Nixon called the Safeguard system.

By no means am I the only Department of Defense official who has come to realize the dilemma of an ever-increasing military power accompanied by an ever-decreasing national security. Nor am I the only defense official to realize that the dilemma cannot be resolved by the development and deployment of ever more complex and more costly machines. Harold Brown said after serving more than four years as DDRE and nearly four years as Secretary of the Air Force:

> Those who have served as civilian officials in the Department of Defense at the level of Presidential appointment . . . have recognized the severely limited utility of military power, and the great risks in its use, as well as the sad necessity of its possession . . . [The] higher their position and, hence, their responsibility, the more they have come to the conclusion that we must seek national security through other than strictly military means . . . and urgently.

In the process of participating in the arms race itself as well as in some of the attempts to bring it under control, I have had the opportunity to watch most of the key men and events from a front-row-center seat. In Part I of this book I will outline the main elements of the arms race, and I will describe in some detail a number of specific instances where I was personally involved. Through them, I shall try to expose some of the principal factors that have driven it forward. I hope to make it clear why I believe that excessive prudence and technological hard-sell have led to an unnecessary overreaction in case after case. And I hope to convince the reader that while these overreactions have produced so far a fairly stable balance of terror between the superpowers, this balance is at a very much higher level of armaments and peril to mankind than would have been the case had a more reasonable approach been followed.

In Part II, I will describe some important current technological trends and programs, including ABM and MIRV. I will try to show why I believe that these threaten to unbalance the balance of terror and that they hold no promise whatever as a means for achieving national security. And lastly, I will share with the reader the reasons for my growing conviction that the end result of it all has been to produce a situation which is at once wondrously absurd and exceedingly dangerous, and which no one, neither the most sanguine weapons fancier nor the most cerebral strategic analyst, ever intended.

PART ONE

Toward
a Balance
of Terror

2

THE RACE BEGINS: NUCLEAR WEAPONS AND OVERKILL

The first atomic bomb was dropped on the Japanese city of Hiroshima on August 6, 1945. At least 66,000 people died immediately as a direct result of the explosion and the fire storm that followed. Tens of thousands more died in the aftermath. About eighty percent of the homes and buildings in Hiroshima were destroyed, and most of the rest were damaged. The bomb weighed nine thousand pounds and was ten feet long and twenty-eight inches in diameter. The explosive it contained was uranium metal highly enriched in the rare isotope U 235. The physical processes of the nuclear explosion took place in less than one one-millionth of a second, and the amount of energy released is estimated to have been about equal to that which would be released in the explosion of fourteen thousand tons of TNT. The bomb was delivered by a B-29 aircraft from the island of Tinian in the Marianas, about fifteen hundred miles from the target. It was exploded several thousands of feet above the ground in order to cover the greatest possible area with high-pressure blast waves and intense heat radiation.

The second atomic bomb was dropped on the Japanese city of Nagasaki on August 9, 1945. At least forty thousand people died immediately from the explosion and the fire storm; many thousands more died in the aftermath. About forty percent of the city's structures were destroyed or very severely damaged. The devastation at Nagasaki was less than that at Hiroshima because of the hilly nature of the terrain and the smaller size of the city. This bomb weighed ten thousand pounds; it was ten feet, eight inches long and five feet in diameter. It used a different explosive, the new, chemical element number 94, plutonium. The explosive equivalent was twenty thousand tons of TNT, or, as this is more commonly described, twenty kilotons (1 kiloton = 1,000 tons).

The Emperor of Japan announced his desire to surrender the next day, August 10, 1945. Soon after, the planned invasion of the Japanese home islands later that same year by a force of millions of men was canceled. It seemed perfectly clear at the time that the two A-bombs had directly resulted in ending the war in the Pacific and that their use had saved, in the net, a great number of lives. The explosion of these bombs was widely celebrated because of this.

Subsequent reviews of what was really going on at that time in Japanese ruling circles have indicated that the situation was more complex than it then seemed. We now know that a peace party, centered around the Emperor himself, had been growing and that the first tentative attempts of this party to end the war predated by many months the detonation of history's first nuclear weapon. The general course of the war in the South Pacific plus the ever-increasing high-explosive-bombing and fire-bombing of Japanese cities in 1945 had steadily strengthened the hand of the peace party. It does still seem most likely that the two atomic bombs were of major importance in finally pushing the whole process over the hump, but this assumption cannot be proved.

These two atomic bombs, plus the test device detonated in the first atomic explosion at Alamogordo, New Mexico, on July 16, 1945, were the product of the Manhattan Project. This project, unique in purpose, style and magnitude, was a child of World War II and of the political and scientific history of the years immediately preceding that conflict.

In 1938, Otto Hahn and Fritz Strassmann, working in Germany and following up on earlier work by Enrico Fermi and his co-workers in Italy, discovered the process known as nuclear fission. When struck by neutrons, the nuclei of certain heavy atoms split roughly in two and, it was later found, released enormous amounts of energy and a few new neutrons in the process. This experimental discovery was soon followed by theoretical explanations, first by Lise Meitner, a German refugee then living and working in Scandinavia, and later by Niels Bohr (a Dane then visiting Princeton) and John A. Wheeler. Enrico Fermi, Leo Szilard (both European refugees then in the United States) and others suggested and soon after confirmed that the fission event took place in such a way as to lead to further fissions under certain special conditions. It was immediately realized that a chain reaction was probably possible and would lead either to enormous explosions or to almost unlimited power production. Szilard, jointly with Eugene Wigner, and later assisted by Edward Teller (all European refugees) then persuaded Albert Einstein (still another) to write a letter to President Franklin D. Roosevelt, bringing all of these possibilities to his attention.

This Einstein letter, dated August 2, 1939, resulted eventually in the creation of the Manhattan Project and in the initiation of the nuclear-arms race. To all of these refugees, and to virtually all other Americans, certainly including me, the politics of the situation were stark and simple: Western civilization was endangered by the twin menaces of Nazism and Fascism—these two unmitigated evils would do anything they could to win and destroy us. Anything that would prevent them from winning had to be good. Winston Churchill said in those days that to stop Hitler he would make an alliance with the Devil.

The Manhattan Project eventually cost two billion dollars, most of it spent in the last two years of the war. In terms of rate and scale and compared with the available national resources then, it was and still remains the largest scientific project of all time, not excepting the Apollo program to land a man on the moon. It was initiated, directed and managed very largely by physical scientists, although the over-all director was a military man, General Leslie Groves, and the production plants were eventually run by professional industrial managers.

The over-all project consisted of a number of subprojects, each directed by physical scientists. J. Robert Oppenheimer directed the Los Alamos Scientific Laboratory in a then secret location on a mesa in New Mexico. There the bombs themselves were designed and fabricated. Ernest O. Lawrence directed the University of California Radiation Laboratory, now named after him. There the electromagnetic process for separating uranium isotopes was perfected; the "rad lab" served as the pilot plant for the huge Y-12 plant at Oak Ridge where the bulk of the uranium exploded over Hiroshima was processed. Harold C. Urey and John Dunning directed the Columbia University project that led to the huge K-25 gaseous-diffusion plant at Oak Ridge for separating uranium isotopes. This plant processed a part of the uranium that went into the Hiroshima bomb, and soon after the war it completely replaced the Y-12 plant and method as a means for producing U 235. Arthur H. Compton, Fermi, Wigner and others directed the work, first at the Metallurgical Laboratory of the University of Chicago and later at the X-10 Laboratory in Oak Ridge that laid the basis for the design and construction of the large production reactors at Hanford, Washington. Ultimately these reactors produced the plutonium for the Nagasaki bomb as well as for the Alamogordo test explosion. Philip H. Abelson directed work on a thermal-diffusion process for separating uranium isotopes. Although it was started quite late, that work too made an important contribution to the total effort. Nearly all of these men, plus a few other scientific leaders, were involved in (though not in control of) the discussions of what to do with the Bomb after it was ultimately produced.

The Manhattan Project showed what American industry

and American science could do when fueled by money, patriotism and fear. It has been held up ever since as a model, very often in situations where it is totally irrelevant. But there are other lessons, too.

At the time, all of us thought we were in a serious and deadly race with the Germans for the atomic bomb. Einstein's August 2, 1939, letter to Roosevelt implied this, and a follow-up letter dated March 7, 1940, said, ". . . interest in uranium has intensified in Germany . . . research there is carried out in great secrecy and . . . has been extended. . . ." The postwar survey of the situation described in Samuel Goudsmit's book *Alsos* showed that we were not in fact in any such race. For a variety of reasons, including a mistaken belief on the part of the Nazis that the war would be very short, lack of interest on the part of many German scientists, and resource allocation problems and internal jealousies, the Germans never mounted a serious effort parallel to the Manhattan Project. It was, however, entirely plausible for us to think that they had. After all, fission had been discovered in Germany, and, despite the fact that many physical scientists had fled from the Nazi regime, it seemed that a sufficient number of competent scientists and engineers remained to initiate and carry out such a project in Europe's most technologically advanced country. Furthermore, the bulk of our intelligence effort was concentrated on classic targets; our technical intelligence was not yet sufficiently extensive and reliable to convince us, by its lack of any real reports about a major program, that such a program did not exist.

The Manhattan Project, then, was based on the first of a long series of mistaken beliefs in our being "raced." Because this was the first such case, our mistake in this regard was, in my view, entirely justified, but our subsequent failure to learn anything from repeatedly making this same mistaken judgment about the existence of a "race" is less so. Time after time since then our leaders have become convinced that the

alent to each other on a per-kiloton basis in their ability to destroy life. The great air raids on Hamburg in 1943, which were carried out entirely with chemical explosives, destroyed about fifty percent of the housing but killed only about three percent of the people. Where atomic weapons were used, the percentage of the area of the cities destroyed and the percentage of the populations killed were more nearly equal. Therefore, we may say that by 1950 we had a stockpile capable of somewhat more than reproducing World War II in a single day.

We might have gone on for years slowly accumulating A-bombs and slowly modifying them in an evolutionary way to fit new types of military equipment, if it had not been for two closely spaced events which caught us completely by surprise and which raised new anxieties and generated new possibilities. These were the first Russian A-bomb test, in August, 1949, and the Korean War, which broke out suddenly in June, 1950. The Russians exploded their atomic bomb much earlier than most American experts had predicted. Up to that time, the Russians had not particularly impressed us by either their scientific or their technological capability, and many experts expected that they would require somewhere between a minimum of five and as much as twenty years before they could duplicate the atomic bomb. Of course, since then Russian accomplishments in missiles and space and in science quite generally have completely changed our estimates of Soviet scientific and technological capability, but we must recall that at the time, in the late 1940s, the general view of the Russians was quite different from what it is today.

We still do not know how much the relatively short gap between the first American and the first Russian explosion was due to successes in Soviet espionage, and how much it was due simply to native Russian capability. At the time it seemed to many of us that espionage must have been far and away the main reason they were able to accomplish the job so quickly, especially after the devastation that had been wreaked on them by World War II. Having since seen some excellent Russian technological progress in other fields, we are no longer quite so sure that this was the case. We should note, furthermore, that it is always easier to do something a second time, even if the only thing known from the first time is that it can be done.

In order to understand the reaction of many Americans to this new Soviet accomplishment and to the breakout of the Korean War, it is necessary to recall that Stalin was still very much alive and that Stalinism was entering one of its more paranoid phases. The Sino–Soviet bloc was newly forged and seemed to most of us in the West (as well as to the leadership of the Soviet Union itself) to be a monolith of tremendous potential power. The surprise and the fear and anxiety generated in this country by these events brought about a number of changes in American life and politics. Of most interest here was the power struggle that developed within the American scientific community over the issue of whether or not to initiate a priority program to develop the H-bomb, or, as it is more properly called, the thermonuclear weapon.

Instead of deriving its energy from nuclear fission, like an A-bomb, an H-bomb derives its energy from a process called thermonuclear fusion. Thermonuclear reactions had been hypothesized by Hans Bethe in the thirties as being the energy source that powers the sun and the stars. For our purposes here we may say that they involve the transformation of various isotopes of hydrogen into isotopes of helium. Sometimes another light element, lithium, plays a role which may be crudely likened in some ways to that of a chemical catalyst. These thermonuclear (or fusion or hydrogen or H-) weapons differ in three very important ways from the earlier fission or A-weapons:

First, the energy released per pound of reactants consumed in thermonuclear explosions is between three and ten times as great as the energy released per pound of reactants consumed in fission explosions.

Second, the materials needed to construct thermonuclear weapons are much cheaper than the materials needed to construct fission weapons. (There is only one exception, tritium, and it is not important just here.)

And third, thermonuclear weapons, unlike fission weapons, may be of practically limitless size and power. The first hydrogen device ever exploded, the Mike Event on November 1, 1952, was a thousand times more powerful than the first atomic bomb, which had been exploded only a little more than seven years earlier. It is now practical to make hydrogen bombs having explosive yields ranging anywhere from ten times the power of a nominal atomic bomb up to ten thousand or more times that amount. The cost of such bombs is, to a first approximation, practically independent of their explosive yield.

The American scientific community, or rather that part of it which was informed about the nuclear-weapons programs of the late forties, was split deeply over the issue of whether or not to go ahead with the development of the H-bomb on a high-priority basis. The numerically smaller side in the split, led by Edward Teller, felt that such a program was the appropriate U. S. reply to the Russian A-bomb and the political realities most recently illustrated by the Korean War. This Teller party admitted that there was as yet no specific promising idea about how to build an H-bomb, but they contended that a project equivalent to the earlier Manhattan Project would inevitably soon generate one. This group also argued that since the Russians had shown they could produce an A-bomb much faster than anticipated we must expect that they could do the same thing with the still hypothetical H-bomb, and that if they did so first the U. S. would suddenly find itself in serious jeopardy.

The other side, led by J. Robert Oppenheimer, opposed the

initiation of a high-priority program on technical, political and moral grounds. They emphasized that none of the proposed general methods for building an H-bomb was at all promising, and they suggested that even if one could be built it would probably involve so much tritium that it would be quite impractical economically, even if technically feasible. (Tritium is the most reactive of the hydrogen isotopes and the only one that is exceedingly expensive. As it finally turned out, large amounts of tritium are not needed.) Further, and partly because there appeared to be no limit to how big an H-bomb could be if one could be built at all, this group felt that the successful development of an H-bomb would lead to a new and very much graver level of danger not only to civilization but to the human race as a whole. Therefore, this group argued, the development of an H-bomb should be avoided if at all possible. A necessary (though clearly not sufficient) step in avoiding such a development was, of course, our refraining from the initiation of a program such as Teller wanted. Oppenheimer was Chairman of the General Advisory Committee of the Atomic Energy Commission at that time, and at a crucial meeting of that body his views were supported by all the members present.

Most politicians, like most scientists, were uninformed about and uninterested in this secret and arcane battle. Of those who were informed and interested, a few, and most of these halfheartedly, supported the Oppenheimer point of view. A larger group very strongly endorsed the views of the Teller party. This group was especially influential, since it included the highest-ranking Air Force officers and civilian officials, plus Lewis L. Strauss, then a member of the Atomic Energy Commission, and some of the key members of the very powerful Joint Congressional Committee on Atomic Energy, notably the Chairman, Senator Brien McMahon, now deceased, and then Representative Henry M. Jackson.

The resulting struggle was presided over at first by President

Truman and then, in its last phase, by President Eisenhower. In January, 1950, President Truman announced his decision that an effort be made to determine the technical feasibility of the thermonuclear weapon. He ordered the AEC and the Defense Department to fix jointly the rate and scale of the program, and he ordered State and Defense to review American foreign policy and military policy in the light of the existing and prospective Soviet nuclear capability. From that point on, the matter was, for all practical purposes, in the hands of the generals and the technologists. They presented a series of *faits accomplis* that really determined what happened next. After most of the major technical and political issues were resolved, but before all the loose ends were neatly tied together, Dwight D. Eisenhower became President of the United States. He appointed Lewis Strauss at first as his Special Assistant for Atomic Energy Matters, and then later, with the advice and consent of the Senate, as Chairman of the U. S. Atomic Energy Commission. In that role, Strauss proceeded to clean up the loose ends with a vengeance.

The drama has been ably and fully described from all points of view by the protagonists themselves as well as by others, some in semifictional form, and I will refrain from giving my own description of it. What matters here is the results of the struggle: (1) the invention of the hydrogen bomb, (2) the establishment of a second nuclear-weapons-development laboratory at Livermore, California, and (3) the defamation of J. Robert Oppenheimer, surely one of the most miserable events in American history and entirely unnecessary to boot, since by that time the first two results had long since been accomplished and the Teller–Strauss view had completely carried the day.

As I mentioned earlier, on the basis of my comprehension of the then existing general political situation, I supported Teller in his efforts to achieve the first of these results, the invention of the hydrogen bomb, and I ended up being the

first director of the Livermore Laboratory, which was the second of these results. However, along with a number of others
who supported the accomplishment of these first two results,
I opposed the prosecution of Oppenheimer. But I protested
neither very loudly in private nor at all in public; I refrained
from doing so for what I think were two good reasons. My
first reason was my special relationship with Ernest O. Lawrence, who, as has been widely reported, quite generally supported Edward Teller in his views on all these matters. Ernest
was my immediate boss and much more besides. I was extremely fond of him and felt I owed everything I was profes-
sionally to him. I still consider myself in a sense to have been
his last student. I absolutely could not do anything which
would add to the burden these problems were already causing
him, and which in fact were making him seriously ill.

My second reason was my relationship with a number of
other good friends and colleagues, including especially Harold
Brown, John Foster, Gerald Johnson, Mark Mills, Arthur
Biehl, Ernest Martinelli, and Kenneth Street, as well as Edward Teller himself. We were all committed to each other in
the task of establishing the Livermore Laboratory. Because of
the Oppenheimer affair and other problems which predated
it, the times were especially difficult and our enterprise was
just then in a particularly delicate condition. An open break
between me and Teller or Strauss would have very seriously
imperiled the whole endeavor, and so I avoided one. I still
think that I did right, considering what the circumstances were
and how I comprehended them, although sometimes on rainy
nights I have some doubts.

The technical development of the H-bomb itself, which
flowed steadily forward despite this maelstrom of political
events, has been described in Teller's book *The Legacy of
Hiroshima* and elsewhere. In May, 1951, the first thermonuclear reaction to take place on earth was produced at Eniwetok
as a part of Operation Greenhouse. The device which pro-

duced it was not in any sense an H-bomb, but the subsequent analysis and study of the physical environment and sequence of events which enabled the reactions to occur led Edward Teller and others at Los Alamos (especially including Stanislaus Ulam) to invent the basic design which then led directly through only one intermediate step to the practical H-bombs of today. This intermediate step was the Mike Event of Operation Ivy. The explosive mechanism was properly called a "device" and was in no sense a practical bomb, but its successful detonation led immediately to the design of devices that were. The first true H-bomb was tested at Bikini in Operation Castle in the spring of 1954. From then until the test moratorium which began in the fall of 1958, subsequent H-bomb and A-bomb tests were largely devoted to developing nuclear explosives for particular applications. Especially important among these were the warheads of the various long-range missiles that were being developed on crash schedules at the same time. Also as a result of technical progress during this period, it became possible to build nuclear weapons of much smaller dimensions and weight. This permitted widespread deployment and dispersal on high-performance tactical aircraft all over the world, which, in turn, increased the danger of unauthorized use. The authorities responded to this danger with still more complicated gadgetry.

Meanwhile, in early August, 1953, midway between Operations Ivy and Castle, and only nine months after the Mike Event, the Soviets exploded their first crude experimental hydrogen device. They too developed this two years later into a variety of practical bombs and warheads. The close spacing of all these events makes it clear that the Russians started a serious H-bomb research and development program at just about the same time we did, perhaps a little before, perhaps a little after. It is still unclear whether or not restraint on our part would have resulted in restraint on their part, though there certainly is no evidence it would have. Nor is it clear whether we really would have lost anything by refraining from going ahead until after they had made a first test. Had we waited, our program would have had much larger and wider support. Such support would most probably have enabled us to catch up easily with the Russians before any politically significant imbalance in the development and deployment of nuclear weapons (both A- and H-bombs) could have developed. In other cases which I will discuss later and which involve both missiles and space vehicles, the overreaction which has occurred whenever we first became aware of their having started something before we did has more than compensated for their earlier start. We have always had plenty of time to block any hypothetical attempt on their part to take advantage of their having started first.

In addition to achieving a thousandfold increase in explosive yield by changing from fission energy to thermonuclear energy, we also increased our destructive capacity by accelerating our unit production rate. We expanded existing plants and constructed new diffusion plants for separating uranium isotopes at Paducah, Kentucky, and Portsmouth, New Hampshire, and new reactors for producing plutonium at Savannah River, South Carolina. By about 1960, we had H-bombs running into the thousands and probably around ten thousand nuclear weapons in all. (By 1964 Senator John O. Pastore was able to say, "We number our weapons in the tens of thousands.") In 1960, John F. Kennedy estimated that the world's nuclear stockpile contained the equivalent of thirty million kilotons, and the Sixth Pugwash Conference used sixty million kilotons as a working assumption. Most of this was in the American stockpile. While most individual weapons were for special purposes such as air defense, tactical applications, and naval uses, the overwhelming bulk of the total explosive power resided in those weapons designed for strategic purposes—that is, for the bombardment of enemy cities and strategic military installations. We are therefore safe in assuming that the United

States possessed at the beginning of the sixties a strategic-weapon stockpile containing twenty to forty million kilotons of explosives, or the energy equivalent of some ten thousand World War IIs, most of which could be released in a matter of hours. We had reached a level of supersaturation that some writers characterized by the word "overkill," an understatement in my opinion. Moreover, we possessed two different but reinforcing types of overkill. First, by 1960 we had many more bombs than they had urban targets, and, second, with a very few exceptions such as Greater Moscow and Greater New York, the area of destruction and intense lethality that a single bomb could produce was very much larger than the area of the targets. Since all or practically all strategic weapons were by then thermonuclear, it is safe to assume that those Soviet or Chinese cities which were equivalent in size and importance to Hiroshima and Nagasaki were, by that time, targets for weapons from one hundred to one thousand times as big as the bombs used in history's only two real demonstrations of what actually happens when large numbers of human beings and their works are hit by nuclear weapons.

The lethality of bombs in the megaton class, due to blast and thermal effects, increases neither directly with the explosive yield nor (as the physics of the explosions might indicate) as the two-thirds power of the yield. Rather, the lethality increases only very slowly in most real applications. But the reason for this is to be found not in the realm of physical phenomena, but in the fact that the size of the bomb has outrun the size of the target and most of the lethal effects are wasted on the sparsely populated areas surrounding the urban centers. Some people may believe, and some officials may argue, that the foregoing is untrue or at the very least irrelevant because our bombs are aimed at "hard military targets" rather than against populations. Unfortunately, such is not really the case, for two reasons: First, certain common military targets such as missile silos will be largely empty when it comes time to launch our weapons if we continue to stick with our present policy of deterrence (i.e., the policy of being ready to launch an unacceptably large second strike in retaliation against anyone who strikes first). Second, many so-called military targets are government and command centers such as Moscow and Peking and Warsaw and other capitals, major transport and communication centers such as Kharkov and Kiev, major seaports such as Leningrad and Vladivostok, and major scientific centers such as Novosibirsk. In short, a list of this second type of so-called military targets is for all practical purposes identical with the list of major population centers, and so any such distinction, even though it is often made, is meaningless. To be sure, there are some military targets which are not parts of major cities and which will not be empty when it is time for retaliation. These include, for example, air defense installations in the Far North, but the relatively small number of weapons which would be diverted to them does not substantially change the picture.

So far we have not considered fallout in this discussion of the holocaust that nuclear war can produce. The details of how heavy the fallout is, where it goes and how soon it comes down depend on such factors as the composition of the bomb, the composition of the soil, the altitude of the burst, and the wind conditions at all levels up to one hundred thousand feet or so. For ground bursts, such as would be used against hard targets or against generally soft targets which unhappily happen to contain a hard target within them, we may conservatively and for convenience assume that for every two kilotons of explosive energy about one square mile will be bathed in lethal levels of radioactive fallout within hours after the explosion. Thus, by about 1960 the two major nuclear powers together possessed stockpiles which could bathe tens of millions of square miles in lethal levels of radioactivity, an area larger than the total land area of the two principals themselves. Of course, the fallout would not be distributed uniformly; some areas would get much more than a lethal dose and others would get less. Also, much of the lethal area would be outside the boundaries of the two powers. For example, an attack on the U. S. industrial heartland running from Chicago along the Great Lakes to the East Coast megalopolis would result in lethal fallout all over southeast Canada, which is where most Canadians live. Beyond this matter of lethal fallout lies the still more ominous matter of genetic and other long-term effects of fallout on the human race as a whole. This is still not fully understood, but appears to be extremely serious. It is this awesome fallout situation which has led to the various dooms-day predictions such as that which was fictionalized in Nevil Shute's *On the Beach*.

If that's where we were in 1960 in nuclear weapons tech-nology and capability, one might ask, what have we been doing since then and why? The answer to this question is that both the U. S. and the U.S.S.R. have continued throughout the sixties to develop, test and stockpile new, often baroque, sometimes rococo, varieties of A-bombs and H-bombs. The testing of these bombs and other nuclear devices has been con-ducted underground except for a brief period extending from late 1961 into 1963. The reason for this is that the Limited Nuclear Test Ban Treaty which came into force in the summer of 1963 prohibits testing anywhere else. China and France are not signatories and have not complied with this prohibition. In the case of the Soviet Union, these tests and developments have included bombs of still greater size than those developed in the fifties. It is generally thought that a Soviet test in 1961 involved a device yielding about sixty megatons. In the case of the United States, weapons development and testing since 1960 have been largely devoted to adapting A-bombs and H-bombs to special purposes and special environments and to making other qualitative improvements, rather than to making them bigger and more powerful. Thus, our test and development program has been directed toward developing bombs which emphasize such special weapons effects as high X-ray yields for use in a hypothetical antimissile defense; to developing techniques for maintaining better command and control over the widely dispersed stockpiles, including especially those in foreign countries; to developing warheads which could better cope with more hostile environments, including very high accelerations and the effects of hypothetical enemy explosions designed to intercept our warheads; and to reducing the size of thermonuclear weapons so that they could be adapted to other special purposes, one of the most important of which is the provision of multiple warheads for a single missile. This last development program goes under the general name of MIRV, an acronym standing for "multiple independently targeted reentry vehicles." Numbers of warheads per missile of more than ten have been mentioned.

One of the political prices paid for getting wide acceptance of the Limited Nuclear Test Ban Treaty in the Congress consisted in a promise by the AEC to conduct an underground-test program vigorous enough to "satisfy all our military requirements." But, clearly, nuclear-weapons tests and experiments conducted underground are more complicated and less productive than they would be if they were held in the atmosphere. It has therefore been judged necessary to conduct such testing at an even faster rate than in the fifties, when aboveground testing was possible. During the sixties the operations at the Nevada test site were conducted on a year-round basis rather than in batches as they were in the forties and fifties.

Also during the sixties our strategic forces changed over from sole dependence on aircraft (in 1960 mostly B-47s and B-52s) to a combination of land-based missiles (now Minutemen and Titans) plus sea-based missiles (now Polarises) plus aircraft (now mostly just B-52s). The missiles deliver a smaller payload than aircraft do, and a larger part of the payload has to be devoted to coping with severe environmental conditions such as those met on reentering the atmosphere or in a near-miss by a hypothetical intercepting explosion. For these reasons, plus the fact that more of our officials had come to appreciate how huge our overkill capability was (even though they may not have used that word), the total yield of our stockpile did not continue to skyrocket upward during the sixties as it had during the fifties. Rather, it probably reached a peak in the early sixties and then either leveled off or began to slowly decrease. However, before anyone breathes a sigh of relief, let me note it is only in the area of total yield and hence total fallout potential that there has been any slowdown in the mad rush toward doomsday. The total number of warheads, and therefore the total number of targets which can be hit, has continued to rise and is about to rise especially rapidly in the near future as a result of the deployment of MIRV. And in the case of the Soviet Union, all of these numbers, including even the total megatons in the stockpile, have been increasing especially rapidly in the last couple of years.

Some, such as Eugene Wigner in his speech to the spring 1969 meeting of the American Physical Society, have seen this decrease in the total megatonnage of our stockpile accompanied by an increase in the total number of individual warheads in our possession as a serious attrition in our over-all capability. This is sometimes referred to as a "virtual attrition" which has been brought about by the Soviet ABM system now deployed around Moscow. The idea here is that whether or not this Soviet ABM system works, the U. S. invention and deployment of MIRV and other penetration devices was prompted by the deployment of the Soviet ABM, and this MIRV deployment is one of the direct causes of the decrease in total megatonnage. It is a fact that our MIRV and other penetration devices (more on these later) were our response to Soviet developments in the ABM field, but even so the concept of "virtual attrition" is basically false, especially in the case of a strategic posture whose purpose is to deter war—that is, to be able to make an unacceptable second, retaliatory strike at the cities and other vitals of the nation which strikes first. The notion of "virtual attrition" is based on the false notion that there is such a thing as a "small nuclear weapon." Small nuclear weapons are like northern Mississippi: there is no such thing, except in a detached theoretical sense. Some parts of Mississippi are, to be sure, farther north than others, and some nuclear weapons are, to be sure, smaller than others; but on a human scale, and compared with the structures that human beings ordinarily build, all A-bombs and H-bombs are very large indeed. In his discussion of this matter, Wigner stated that the present single ten-megaton warhead now carried by the Titan was to be replaced by a MIRV warhead consisting of ten individual nuclear warheads of fifty kilotons explosive power each, and he bemoaned what he calculated to be a loss in the lethality of the system. I know of no plan to do any such thing; apparently Wigner had become confused by plans for equipping the Navy's Poseidon missile with a MIRV such as he described. In any case, there simply is no fundamental reason for such a large change (twentyfold) in the yield to occur when single warheads are replaced by MIRVs. Some small decrease is inevitable, but the total area covered by some given blast level is not necessarily reduced; on the contrary, it normally increases somewhat.

Even so, let us suppose Wigner's notion about the plans for a MIRV for Titan were true. Each of those ten 50-kiloton warheads is almost four times as big as the warhead which gutted Hiroshima and killed nearly one hundred thousand people in the process. Except in the narrowest technocratic interpretation, it makes absolutely no sense to call such bombs small. Unless, perhaps, either Moscow or Leningrad is the target, the imaginary Titan MIRV (i.e., the real Poseidon) is deadlier and more vicious than the real single-warhead Titan.

Between 1950 and 1960, the explosive yields of nuclear weapons changed a thousandfold, the means for delivering them (subsonic aircraft) changed rather little, and the number of persons in the Sino–Soviet bloc who were "at risk" to the U. S. strategic forces changed from a few million to a few hundred million, or by about a hundredfold. Between 1960 and 1970, the explosive yields of nuclear weapons changed very little, the speed of the delivery systems increased thirtyfold (from subsonic aircraft to supersonic Mach-25 intercontinental rockets), but the number of persons in China and the U.S.S.R. who were at risk remained more or less a few hundred million. The reason for the lack of a significant increase in the number of persons at risk during the second decade, as contrasted with the huge increase during the first decade, is obvious: it is the supersaturated, or "overkill," capacity we reached in about 1960. This static situation has been maintained now for almost ten years despite all the breakthroughs and other technological advances that took place during the sixties, and we may therefore reasonably expect that new breakthroughs and deployments of new types of weapons in the near future will similarly produce little or no change in the number of persons at risk on either side. However, as we shall see, the situation has worsened in other ways. And, unless some large change happens, we can expect it to continue to do so.

3

THE BOMBER BONANZA

At the same time that America was pursuing its spectacular accumulation of nuclear weapons, it was devoting considerable attention to perfecting the means of delivering them. At first this effort naturally focused on the bomber.

The strategic bombardment of Germany in World War II by the United States Army Air Force was carried out largely with B-17s and B-50s. These subsonic propeller-driven aircraft flew at speeds of a couple of hundred miles per hour. They could carry payloads weighing a few tons for distances ranging up to a thousand miles or so. They dropped the bulk of the 2.7 megatons of chemical high explosives which were showered on Germany during the latter part of the war. The bombardment of Japan, including the fire-bombing of Tokyo and other major cities and the delivery of the two atomic bombs, was carried out with B-29s, another type of subsonic propeller-driven aircraft. These had been especially designed for the Pacific campaign, where a much longer range was needed than in the European campaign.

Aircraft continued after World War II and up until 1960 to be the sole means of delivery for our strategic weapons. And even in 1970 the great bulk of the total megatonnage in our nuclear stockpile is still programmed for delivery by aircraft. After World War II the B-36 bomber, an extremely long-range propeller-driven aircraft, was introduced into the force to give us a home-based intercontinental strategic bombardment capability. In keeping with the general development of aviation, both civil and military, all of these propeller aircraft were eventually replaced by the B-47 and the B-52 jet bombers.

The first American jet bomber, the B-47, was introduced into the Air Force inventory in the late forties. It did not have either the desired range or the desired payload-carrying capability, and so a still larger airplane, the B-52, was designed specifically to meet these needs. The B-52 was simply a much larger version of the B-47. Both have speeds in the high subsonic range (about six hundred miles per hour). The B-52 began to be phased into the force in 1954. Today the largest part of our strategic stockpile in terms of total explosive power is still programmed to be delivered by one of the later models of this same B-52.

The B-58 was designed in the early fifties to meet the desire for a plane capable of supersonic speeds over enemy territory. It became operational in the late fifties and obsolete in the late sixties. This aircraft was programmed to fly most of the distance from its home base to a target at subsonic speeds, and then to dash in over the target and out again at about twice the speed of sound. The inventory of these airplanes never became very large, and consequently they never played a major role in our strategic-delivery plans.

In addition to gradual progress in the development of airframes and aircraft propulsion systems, the years since World War II have seen further developments in devices to confuse air defenses (electronic countermeasures and chaff), in weapons designed to roll back the defenses, and in the development of "standoff" weapons. These last include various types of small pilotless aircraft and guided rockets. These can be launched directly from the B-52s, and they can then fly ahead on their own for hundreds of additional miles, making it unnecessary for the aircraft themselves to penetrate all the way to the immediate target area. The longest-range missile of this type ever to be seriously considered was the famous Skybolt missile, which after several years of on-again, off-again and development effort, was finally canceled at the beginning of the Kennedy administration.

Since the first plane rolled off the production line in 1954, the B-52 has gone through a series of major model changes. Some of these changes resulted from modification in operational concepts and requirements. But most of them resulted from the steady advance of the technological state of the art in engine design, aerodynamic design, and "avionics" (a general term coined to cover all of the various electronic devices carried by modern aircraft for communications, navigation, weapons control, defense penetration, etc.). As a result, the B-52G's and the B-52H's (the last one came off the line in 1962) were very different from the original B-52A. In fact, the difference between the B-52H and the B-52A was almost as great as the difference between the B-52A and the B-47.

Except for the B-58, no entirely new strategic bombardment aircraft has been introduced since the B-52. The reason for this has not been a lack of ideas, but rather that attention since the mid-fifties has been primarily focused on an entirely new kind of intercontinental delivery system, the long-range ballistic missile to be discussed later. Nevertheless, the Air Force has continued to propose several new radically different types of aircraft. Because of what their stories reveal about the dynamics of the arms race, two are especially worthy of mention: the huge supersonic B-70 and the nuclear airplane, or the ANP, as it was usually called.

The B-70 program was initiated in the late 1950s. Only two prototype aircraft were ever built. These were flown in the mid-sixties, and the program is now dormant. The plane was to be capable of flight at Mach 3 (i.e., at three times the speed of sound, or about two thousand miles per hour), to fly at altitudes in the neighborhood of 100,000 feet and to carry payloads of many tons to targets anywhere in the world. Its gross weight at takeoff would have been over 500,000 pounds. The airframe was to have been constructed of titanium and stainless steel, since the aluminum alloys used for all other aircraft would not stand up under the extreme temperatures generated on the leading surfaces at such high speeds.

The history of the B-70 is closely linked to the political and technological environment of the era.

The program began in the mid-fifties as a study of what was then called the WS-110. By early 1957, development work (mostly done at the old NACA laboratories) on the various kinds of components and design ideas necessary for long-range supersonic flight had reached a point where it became clear to everyone concerned that a Mach-3 airplane of intercontinental range could really be built. As a result, in mid-1957 the Air Force authorized both Boeing and North American Aviation to engage in a competitive design study.

Meanwhile, the huge programs to develop the intercontinental ballistic missiles, or ICBMs, had been started and had been given the highest national priority. As we will see, they soon came to dominate the technological scene in the U. S., and they absorbed the bulk of the resources, including both men and money, which the Air Force could devote to research and development. Thus, even if the studies showed the project practicable, it was not likely that the U. S. would be able to commit the necessary resources to it. But on October 4, 1957, shortly after the study started, Sputnik, the first artificial earth satellite, was launched into space by the U.S.S.R. The political atmosphere both in Washington and throughout the country was transformed by the sudden shock of discovering that the United States was not automatically first in technological feats of that sort. Frightened by the Soviets' apparent technical superiority, Americans were disposed to listen sympathetically to anybody with an advanced-technology program to sell.

Thus, when North American Aviation was selected as the prime contractor for the project at the end of 1957, the firm was ordered by the Air Force to proceed on a high-priority basis with the development of what had become known by then as the B-70. The official priority rating given was just below that of the ballistic-missile development program. The B-70 appealed particularly to the flying generals, who did not look forward to becoming "the silent silo-sitters of the sixties." They took a different view from those who advocated the primacy of the ICBMs. General Curtis E. LeMay, the man with the cigar, was the commander of the Strategic Air Command (SAC) at the time. As I recall his personal view of the priorities, he placed the B-52H first (it was then called the B-52 Squared) and the B-70 second (it was then called the WS-110). The nuclear airplane (ANP) was somewhere in the middle of his short list, and the long-range missiles were at the bottom. He and other leading Air Force generals managed to make it clear to the contractor that they personally considered the B-70 to be at least as important as the ICBMs, whatever the official priorities might be, and they ordered first flight by the end of 1961.

Before the first full year under contract was over, there were more than forty first- and second-tier subcontractors, and approximately two thousand vendors and suppliers were by then involved in the total program. Seventy of the then ninety-six United States Senators had a major part of the program in their states, and something like a majority of the Congressional districts had at least one supplier of consequence.

Many different arguments in favor of the B-70 program were presented by its proponents to the Congress and in the aviation and missile press. It was said that, as compared with conventional bombardment aircraft, its speed gave it certain very important advantages: it could respond much faster, it could arrive in the target area much sooner, and it could penetrate air defenses more surely. Compared with missiles, its main advantages were said to reside in its greater "flexibility." That is, like any other aircraft, it could be launched into the air very soon after receiving a warning and it could be easily recalled if the warning turned out to be a false alarm. It could carry out a search-and-destroy mission on arrival in the target area, and it could deliver larger weapons with greater accuracy than was generally foreseen for missiles. In addition, the claim was made that it could also be useful for such purposes as "showing the flag" and serving as a high-velocity platform for launching artificial earth satellites. In this latter application, it could in theory substitute for some other non-recoverable rocket first stages, such as the Atlas or Titan booster. Because of its enormous speed and great flight altitude and these other real and hypothetical advantages, it was sometimes called the "manned missile."

At the time the contract for building the B-70 was awarded to North American in 1957, the multistage intercontinental ballistic missiles, or ICBMs, were still in a very early test phase, and the single-stage intermediate-range ballistic missiles, or IRBMs (Jupiter and Thor), had been successfully launched for the first time only months before. The first Atlas B, with all engines operating, would not be launched until some months after the B-70 program was initiated, and even then only to less than half of its intercontinental range. The guidance and control systems for these long-range missiles were also still in a very early stage of flight test. Although some of the leaders in this field, particularly Stark Draper of M.I.T.'s Instrument Laboratory, were predicting extreme accuracies down the road, it was reasonable to believe then that aircraft delivery accuracy would continue to be very significantly better than missile delivery accuracy. Hence, the B-70 received its priority go-ahead at the time when advanced-technology programs generally received a friendly welcome from the Congress and the people, and when its technical competition was still in too early a development stage to offer a sufficiently convincing alternative.

By the end of 1958, though, an Atlas-D missile had reached a range of four thousand miles, and the first field test of an operational missile was conducted in September, 1959. By October, 1959, some $300 million had already been spent on the B-70, and many hundreds of millions more were scheduled to be spent during the remainder of that fiscal year (i.e., through June of 1960). The Air Force was asking for an additional $460 million for the next fiscal year. In the budget planning for fiscal year 1961, which took place as usual six to nine months before its beginning—that is, during the last three months of calendar year 1959—we pared this figure back in the Office of the Secretary of Defense to about $360 million. We then discussed this and other development programs with representatives of the Bureau of the Budget and with Dr. George B. Kistiakowsky (then the President's Special Assistant for Science and Technology), and it soon became evident that there was rising opposition in the White House staff to spending anything like these amounts on this program. In a later meeting with President Eisenhower himself at his vacation headquarters in Georgia, it was finally decided that we should cut the program all the way back to an annual level of $75 million for the fiscal year beginning July, 1960, and that we should reduce expenses immediately for the remainder of the then current fiscal year so as to reach that goal in a rational manner. Such a program level would allow exploratory development work on components and certain advanced subsystems, but it would eliminate the construction of any prototypes, and, of course, indefinitely postpone any deployment plans. North American Aviation received an order from the Air Force to this effect in early December of 1959.

An intense campaign to save the B-70 was immediately launched in the Congress, in the aviation and missile press, and on a wider front in the general media. All kinds of visions of potential national dangers (and, just incidentally, lost jobs) were conjured up. Carl Vinson of Georgia, the chairman of the House Armed Services Committee, said, ". . . by cutting back the B-70 we have increased the danger to our survival . . ." Senator Barry Goldwater, who was a brigadier general in the Air Force Reserve, personally appealed the case to President Eisenhower. Senator Clair Engle, Democrat of California, and also an officer in the Air Force Reserve, characterized the cutbacks as a "blunder which may have the gravest consequences to our national security," and he claimed that the B-70 was needed to make up for what he said was the "five-year lead of Soviet missile developments." Even so, the lower budgetary level was maintained throughout the first half of 1960.

Then, during the 1960 campaign for the Presidency, the B-70 was given a brief new lease on life. Even before the new fiscal year started, on July 1, 1960, about $60 million had been tacked onto the originally planned $75 million. This extra money was supposed to be used for development work on some of the most critical weapons subsystems; and in combination with other readjustments in the project, it was to make possible the construction of a single prototype aircraft. However, a program leading to only one prototype never made sense, and going through such a step was nothing more than an exercise in salami tactics. Thus, in August, another $20 million was added for a second plane. Then, just days before the Nixon–Kennedy election contest in November, 1960, the Department of Defense announced that it was bringing the total B-70 budget for the then current fiscal year up to $265 million. As a result of these increased funds, the number of airplanes to be built was increased to four for sure, with eight more possible, and the four were to be prototypes of a "usable weapon system." In California, the announcement of this new lease on life was accompanied by a detailed statement by North American Aviation about the recent sad history of declining employment in southern California and how these funds would change all that.

Although Nixon did carry California in 1960, Kennedy won

nationally, and the B-70's new lease on life ran out almost immediately. Shortly after the inauguration, I, along with Secretary McNamara, Jerome Wiesner, then Kennedy's science adviser, David Bell, the new Director of the Budget, and a few others, attended a meeting with the new President where the outlines of Kennedy's first defense program were developed. By the time of that meeting long-range missiles of several different types had been successfully flown, sufficient reliability and accuracy had been demonstrated, several models of missiles were already deployed, and the first Minuteman (a *second*-generation ICBM) had just been test-flown successfully. And, no doubt most important, the new Administration had confirmed the claims of the prior one that the missile gap for all practical purposes did not exist and had stopped claiming that it did. As a result, the B-70 program was cut back once again, this time to one which would produce two prototype aircraft but no more. When President Kennedy announced this decision, Senator Goldwater immediately denounced it and said that it would "go down in history as one of our worst tactical blunders." Other members of the Congress, including especially some from California, made similar statements. And the Los Angeles County Board of Supervisors passed a motion urging the Administration "to reimplement the program for mass construction of the B-70 supersonic bomber." The Board duly noted that "much of the work of constructing these bombers would be done by Los Angeles area concerns."

Over the next three years, a battle of growing intensity raged between the executive branch and the Congress over the B-70. McNamara requested an appropriation of about $200 million annually for the program and stated that his objective was to build two prototype aircraft. Characteristically, the Air Force generals made it known that that was not their objective, and the Congress, inspired especially by Chairman Carl Vinson of the Armed Services Committee, appropriated or tried to appropriate about $300 million more per year than the Secretary of Defense requested. It also tried to convert the program to one committed to produce about two hundred so-called reconnaissance-strike bombers at a cost usually estimated by friends of the B-70 at $10 billion. It was not for naught that the generals and the admirals referred to the chairman as "Uncle Carl."

For a time the argument was raised to the level of a constitutional issue. At one point Vinson said in a speech, "What is Congress's function in defense? Is it a partner? Does it have a voice? Or is it just a Mr. Moneybags, to give or withhold funds? That's not what the Constitution says; the Constitution grants the Congress the exclusive power to raise and support and make rules for our military forces."

I think those were, in the abstract, very good questions. Unfortunately, though, the real issue was then not so much about the merits of and need for the B-70 as over the question of military versus civilian control of defense planning. It was not until years later, in the 1969 ABM debates, that the Congress got around to arguing the real merits of an important weapons system, and, in the process, declined to accept the word of either the civilian secretariat or the generals as gospel. (Like the B-70 dispute, the TFX controversy which raged during the middle sixties was largely over the issue of civilian versus military control.)

But McNamara, with the support of the President, stood his ground and refused to spend the extra funds on the B-70, even when they were fully authorized and appropriated as an integral part of the final defense budget.

The program did finally work out middling well in a technical sense. Two prototypes were built, and the first of them flew in September, 1964. In another flight a year later, a speed of Mach 3—two thousand miles per hour—was reached and maintained for two minutes during a 107-minute, 1,900-mile flight out of Edwards Air Force Base in California. One of the two proto B-70s was destroyed in a tragic collision with an accompanying F-104 during a test flight on June 8, 1966. The other made its last flight in February, 1969, when it flew cross country to Dayton, Ohio, to take its place in a museum.

It is important to emphasize that the B-70 was not terminated because North American was not doing a good job, nor because the B-70 could not be successfully built, nor because it had *none* of the advantages claimed for it. Its fatal problems were two: first, the very great cost of these hypothetical advantages (250 B-70s, which is the size of the fleet the Air Force at one time considered for the 1965–1975 time period, would surely have cost well over $10 billion), and, second, the eventually clearly demonstrated successful development of intercontinental missiles. It is, however, entirely possible that at some future date, when weaknesses in our missile forces, now only dimly foreseen, become clear, a new program for an advanced manned strategic aircraft may be initiated. And it is equally possible that it may be designed to fly at Mach 3.

4

THE ELUSIVE
NUCLEAR AIRPLANE

The story of the nuclear airplane is entirely different from the story of the B-70, and a review of that ill-starred program can reveal a great deal about some of the basic forces that drive the arms race. The idea of the nuclear airplane dates back to the waning days of World War II and involves a wedding of two of the technologies which burst forth on the world in the early forties: jet propulsion and nuclear power.

An ordinary jet engine, such as those which propel the large commercial transport aircraft of today, is, in principle, a fairly simple and straightforward device. Air is taken in through a scoop at the front end, compressed by a fan and then mixed with fuel. This mixture then burns and heats itself and in so doing greatly increases its pressure. It then pushes its way toward the rear end of the jet, turning a turbine in the process and finally being exhausted at high speed through a nozzle, giving the aircraft a push in the opposite direction. The turbine extracts some of the energy from the heated air and uses it to drive the compressor fan. The power plant for a nuclear aircraft is, in principle, very similar. Instead of heating the air by mixing kerosene or gasoline with it and then burning the mixture, the air is heated by the energy produced in a nuclear reactor. There are two basic schemes for accomplishing this. In one scheme the air passes directly through the reactor itself and is heated on direct contact with fuel elements consisting of uranium metal which has been clad or "canned" in some suitable material. In the other, heat is removed from the reactor by some intermediate fluid (such as liquid sodium) and taken to another heat transfer unit (crudely similar to an ordinary automobile radiator), where it is transferred from the intermediate fluid to the air, and then the intermediate fluid (the radiator water in an auto) goes back to the reactor for more heat. The first of these schemes is called the direct cycle, and the second is called the indirect cycle.

Work on the nuclear airplane began at an annual rate of $1.3 million in fiscal 1946 and grew steadily to $8.3 million in fiscal 1951. At first only Air Force funds were involved, but by 1949 the AEC had a major piece of the action, which it kept through the end of the program in 1961. The Navy was also involved, but only to a much smaller degree. From the beginning the program had an unusually stormy career. In addition to being beleaguered by extremely difficult technical problems, it was surrounded by political controversy and buffeted by various political power struggles. The program budget oscillated; decisions for early flight of one kind or another were made and quickly rescinded; the AEC concerned itself with what was the Defense Department's business and vice versa; the JCAE, the Joint Committee on Atomic Energy, repeatedly tried to usurp the prerogatives of the executive branch; and through it all the Air Staff and certain major contractors tried to exploit every little bit of confusion and animosity that arose.

Research on the project was begun by the Fairchild Engine and Aircraft Company in 1946 under the rubric of NEPA (Nuclear Energy for the Propulsion of Aircraft). In the next two years, a series of committees urged the project on with glowing testimonials to its importance and optimistic predictions about its possibilities. The Research and Development Board of the Defense Department recommended that it proceed on a priority basis under the supervision of the board and the AEC. The Congressional Aviation Policy Board reported to Congress that NEPA deserved "the highest priority in atomic-energy research and development." An M. I. T. report commissioned by the AEC contended that the nuclear aircraft was feasible and could probably be achieved within fifteen years. (All the early laboratory work and virtually all the theoretical studies were focused on the direct-cycle approach. This was more straightforward and seemed then to offer the surest means for flight in the foreseeable future. Research work on the indirect cycle was not undertaken until 1954.)

Such optimism was not borne out by the initial findings of the researchers. A number of very difficult problems very soon became evident. It turned out that there were then no materials available which would (1) stand up to the high-intensity nuclear radiation which necessarily existed throughout the interior of the reactor, (2) resist corrosion by the very hot air which passed through the reactor at great speed, and (3) be guaranteed not to leak any of the highly radioactive fission products into the exhaust airstream.

It also soon became painfully clear that there was a very difficult shielding problem. As with other high-power nuclear reactors, it was necessary to surround this one with a heavy shield in order to protect the pilots, and any instruments or other cargo which the airplane might be carrying, from the intense radiation always generated by these devices. The shielding problem is especially difficult in this case because the shield must be light enough to be flown and because it must be pierced in such a way as to allow large masses of air to pass through it at high speed without creating too large a radiation leak.

A third, very basic set of problems was related to potential operating hazards such as would obviously be associated with a crash landing of such an airplane or even with lesser accidents. While most of the intellectual effort devoted to solving these problems was of the usual serious and straightforward kind, occasionally some bizarre proposals arose. One which was discussed quite seriously was that older men (i.e., men beyond the usual age for begetting children) should be used as pilots so that genetic damage from radiation would be held at a minimum and because older people are generally more resistant to radiation than younger ones.

However, these problems did not daunt those who wanted to have a nuclear plane in flight as soon as possible. At the end of 1950 the Defense Department recommended that the project aim to put a subsonic aircraft in the air in 1956 or 1957. The project passed from feasibility studies into the development phase. The General Electric Company was commissioned to develop a propulsion plant (using the direct cycle), and General Dynamics was contracted to conduct the "flying testbed" program with the aim of achieving a first flight by 1957. The Joint Committee on Atomic Energy, which eventually held more than thirty-six hearings on the subject, soon became the most vigorous and vocal supporter of the early-flight scheme. It insisted that the Air Force support the program on a massive scale, sufficient to insure success, or abandon it entirely.

The political pressure to put a plane in flight as soon as possible eventually proved fatal to the program. The part of the program which was supposed to develop reactor materials had by no means reached the point where it could be certain of coming up with something suitable. By demanding that a flight reactor be designed immediately regardless of whether anyone knew how to do so, the politicians and bureaucrats severely inhibited real progress in this vital area. As I will argue, politicians should in general take a strong role in weighing the over-all value of technological programs. But in this particular case, politicians insisted on meddling deeply in the strictly technical elements of the program, and the practically inevitable result was a serious retardation.

In July of 1952 the AEC and the Defense Department announced plans for a flight test of a nuclear-propulsion system between 1956 and 1958 which would use a modified conventional airplane as a "testbed." By then it was widely apparent that no one knew how to build a nuclear engine that could propel an aircraft on its own, but rather than go back to the drawing board the directors bullheadedly insisted on flying something anyway, even if the new device was little more than a passenger in a conventionally powered aircraft.

After Eisenhower's inauguration, all major development programs were reevaluated, including what was by then known as ANP (Aircraft Nuclear Propulsion), and for a while it looked as if good sense might prevail. In March, 1953, an ad hoc committee of the Air Force Scientific Advisory Board recommended cutting the program back fifty percent, on the ground that the production activities were premature in the light of the slow rate of progress in research. The following month the National Security Council urged that the program be canceled entirely. Secretary of Defense Charles Wilson issued orders to that effect, calling the nuclear airplane a "shitepike." The "flying testbed" program was terminated, along with most of the work on the direct-cycle propulsion system, and the program was reoriented toward basic research.

Yet only seven months later the ANP enthusiasts were back in action. The Air Force repeatedly told the AEC that it was once again interested in the ANP and asked it to expedite the experimental work. In April, 1954, the director of the ANP project, Air Force General Donald Keirn, claimed that the nuclear-propelled aircraft could be put in flight in half the time originally foreseen, if it were given high priority. The JCAE immediately called for a "crash effort" on the program. At the same time the Pratt and Whitney Corporation was commissioned to begin research on an indirect-cycle propulsion system.

In early 1955, the AEC reported that progress on the direct-cycle system had surpassed expectations and authorized additional funds for it. The Defense Department and the AEC agreed to accelerate the program, with the objective of testing a prototype propulsion plant about 1959. The Air Force insisted that this was a realistic goal. Competition for airframe studies was opened, and General Electric and Pratt and Whitney were directed to proceed with their work on the propulsion systems.

The Joint Committee continued to receive optimistic predictions from the Air Force. In June, 1956, General Curtis LeMay, then commander of SAC, testified that an early flight by a nuclear aircraft was both necessary and possible. The following month, General Keirn told the committee that a ground test of a propulsion system would be possible in 1959, with a flight the following year.

But a review of the technical progress in the program and subsequent budget cuts by the Defense Department led to postponing the flight target date by eighteen months. In December an experimental reactor operated a turbojet in a laboratory for several hours, but not at a temperature suitable for flight propulsion. The accelerated flight program was again canceled, and the research efforts were cut back.

After reviewing the matter, the Air Force Scientific Advisory Board recommended again that less emphasis be put on designing the plane until a suitable reactor had been developed, but the Joint Committee continued to urge the earliest possible flight. Deputy Defense Secretary Donald Quarles agreed with the Air Force Advisory Board that no date should be set for flight until the reactor had been developed. This was an eminently sensible conclusion in my view, but it was not to the liking of the Joint Committee, which continued in letters and testimony to insist to the Defense Department on the importance of immediate flight. In May, 1957, another advisory board, chaired by Air Force General William Canterbury, recommended that a low-level nuclear plane be developed. The reason for specifying a low-level plane was simple: no one knew how to design a reactor suitable for any other kind of flight. Anxious to hold back the budget as much as possible, some Administration officials fought the project, but the Joint Committee, backed up by still another advisory-committee report and a letter from Air Force Secretary James H. Douglas, fought for it. In July, Secretary Quarles relented and approved a program aiming at a test flight in the mid-sixties.

As usual during such periods of political buffeting, little technical progress was made. The date for the test flight was again put off, and complaints were heard that Pratt and Whitney could not carry on adequate research on the indirect cycle effectively without more funds.

At this point the first Sputnik went into orbit, and the Sputnik psychology affected the ANP program just as it did all other high-technology projects. Representative Melvin Price, Chairman of the Research and Development Subcommittee of the JCAE, wrote President Eisenhower that an early flight program was desirable both for military reasons and as a psychological victory to counteract the effects of Sputnik. The AEC recommended that early flight of a nuclear plane be pursued as a means of increasing American scientific prestige in the post-Sputnik era. The Air Force and several Defense Department officials threw their support to the direct-cycle propulsion system in hopes that flight could be achieved as soon as possible, this time suggesting the early sixties as a flight goal.

Eisenhower requested his science adviser, James Killian, to investigate the recommendations, and Killian appointed Robert Bacher to chair a study committee on the matter. The Bacher Committee reiterated the earlier recommendation against accelerating an early flight program and urged that the ANP effort concentrate on developing a suitable reactor. The President expressed agreement with this view. But General

Keirn, the Joint Committee, and Congressional ANP proponents attacked the Bacher report and continued to press their
case.

When I became Director of Defense Research and Engineering in 1958, by the terms of the position, the ANP program would have come under my jurisdiction; but because of
the long, difficult, contentious history of the program, Deputy
Secretary Quarles chose to continue himself in direct charge
while I was beginning to take up my other responsibilities.

As a result of lack of progress and negative reports on the
project, Quarles backed away from his July, 1957 position
approving a test flight in the mid-sixties. He continued to maintain this new position despite strong pressures from the Air
Force, the AEC, and the Joint Committee, and in the face
of very strong lobbying on the part of the larger contractors.
A few months later, Quarles died suddenly and I assumed responsibility for overseeing the program. (The claim was made
shortly after Quarles's death that at a meeting in the afternoon
before he died he had had a change of mind and had told
someone that he wanted to go ahead with a flight vehicle. Unfortunately, Quarles made no written record of this. I was at
the meeting; I recall he was beginning to yield to the enormous
pressures being applied in favor of early flight, but I do not
believe he had quite yet finally decided what to do.)

After carefully reviewing the program with Arthur T. Biehl
and others on my staff, I determined that the program objectives for the immediate future should be to (a) continue the
development of only such reactors and power plants as would
be suitable for militarily useful nuclear flight; (b) increase
the effort on the indirect-cycle program so as to determine its
potentialities at an earlier date than previously contemplated;
and (c) defer initiation of a specific flight program until one
of the advanced power plants was established as feasible and
potentially useful, and until a flight program could be insti-

tuted without seriously interfering with the development of militarily useful power plants.

This decision was very poorly received by those who wanted to "go full steam ahead, damn the technical minutiae," and in the following general questioning by committee members I was very closely cross-examined about my views. The hearings were especially remarkable in that the heads of the contractor programs, D. Shoults of the General Electric Corporation, B. A. Schmickrath of the Pratt and Whitney Corporation, and Andrew Kalitinsky of the Convair Corporation, were also brought in to testify. Shoults and Schmickrath presented prepared statements to the committee, and all three responded to the general questioning of the committee members. To put it simply, Mr. Shoults was there specifically for the purpose of rebutting some of the government witnesses and to testify in behalf of expanding a program which he managed and for which his corporation was receiving approximately $100 million per year.

A more intensive, continuing review of the program in the course of next year revealed that during all this political maneuvering, while there had been substantial progress in the rate of spending money, there had been precious little progress toward solving the basic problems which had been recognized by 1948, well over a decade earlier. After all that time and effort, there were still no materials available with which a useful propulsion reactor unit could be built, the problem of crew and cargo shielding had still not been satisfactorily solved, and potential hazards to the public associated with potential accidents of various kinds were still as bad as ever. The kind of airplane that could perhaps be built and the kinds of uses to which the airplane could conceivably be put appeared to be of no value at all. It was claimed that if we would only build such an airplane and get on with the flight program, somehow in due course these problems would be solved. However, since over ten years of intensive laboratory work by some pretty good people had failed to make any real progress at all on these problems, we saw no reason to believe that exposing the reactor prototype then under construction to still more hostile environments (vibrations, etc.) would be useful in solving them.

Therefore, just as the Eisenhower administration was coming to a close, we (my staff and I) determined to terminate further work on the direct cycle and to continue only fairly fundamental work on the indirect cycle at Pratt and Whitney at a level of approximately $25 million per year. I reported all of this to Secretary Gates, but, since it was so late, he suggested that I talk it over with the incoming secretariat. I then discussed the whole matter with Roswell Gilpatric, the Deputy Secretary of Defense designate, and also with Jerome Wiesner, who was about to become President Kennedy's Special Assistant for Science and Technology. If there was any difference between Wiesner's views and mine, he felt more negatively about the program, and, as a result, ANP was canceled in the first months of the Kennedy administration. More precisely, it was not totally canceled: research in the indirect cycle at Pratt and Whitney, essentially along the lines of my earlier recommendation to Secretary Gates, was in fact continued, but under a different rubric.

All during the last two years of the life of this program, the public was bombarded by scare stories and by self-serving intelligence revelations about how the Soviets were just on the verge of accomplishing an ANP of their own and about how dreadful it would be for us if we didn't have one, too. Representative Melvin Price, Chairman of the JCAE subcommittee holding the hearings, commented on "the shattering impact of Russia's Sputniks last fall" and said:

> it became evident that we could ill-afford another humiliating psychological defeat in the eyes of the world. Our views were reinforced by our talks with

Russian scientists in Moscow last fall, who confirmed that the Soviets were, indeed, pursuing a vigorous development program for a nuclear-powered aircraft.

Later, in the letter to President Eisenhower, Congressman Price wrote: ". . . recent events including the launching of an earth satellite by the Soviet Union have lent urgency to the long-standing need for the United States to develop a flying capability in the field of nuclear-propelled aircraft."

Senator Richard B. Russell of Georgia said in a television statement:

> The report that the Russians have test-flown an atomic-powered aircraft is an ominous new threat to world peace, and yet another blow to the prestige and security of our nation and the free world. It follows in tragic sequence the Russian success of last fall in launching the first earth satellite. If the report is true, it means that we are today faced with a new weapon of terrifying consequences. A plane powered by nuclear energy could have practically unlimited range and load capacity and therefore would be a weapon of incalculable danger to us.

General Keirn (who headed the ANP office) said in a speech, "This emphasis [in the last year] on technical progress has resulted in many suggested proposals to accelerate the ANP program in an effort to beat the Russians to first nuclear flight." In another speech General Keirn said:

> I'm sure each of you is aware of and appreciates the seriousness of any potential threat to our seacoast military installations and industrial and population centers posed by a large enemy submarine

fleet. Imagine in addition to this a fleet of "enemy" high-speed aircraft continuously patrolling the air space just outside our early-warning net capable of air-launching a devastating missile attack followed by high-speed penetration or attack against our hardened installations.

A letter from an employee of one of the contractors was published by the Joint Committee in the record of the hearing; it said:

I believe that an overwhelming majority of American citizens would prefer to be absolutely sure that the amount of national defense available is adequate for security rather than risk even a momentary period of potential collapse in retaliatory deterrent. The nuclear aircraft program can help prevent this potential collapse.

The December 1, 1958, issue of *Aviation Week* carried a signed editorial which said:

On page 28 of this issue we are publishing the first account of Soviet nuclear powered bomber prototype along with engineering sketches in as much detail as available data permits. Appearance of this nuclear powered military prototype comes as a sickening shock to the many dedicated U. S. Air Force and Naval aviation officers, Atomic Energy Commission technicians, and industry engineers who have been working doggedly on our own nuclear aircraft propulsion program despite financial starvations, scientific scoffing, and top level indifference, for once again the Soviets have beaten us needlessly to a significant technical punch.

The story on page 28, datelined Washington and entitled "Soviets Flight Testing Nuclear Bomber," stated flatly:

A nuclear powered bomber is being flight tested in the Soviet Union. Completed about six months ago, this aircraft has been observed both in flight and on the ground by a wide variety of foreign observers from communist and non-communist countries.

There followed all kinds of purported details and even some sketches in which large red stars showed plainly in the side view and the top view of the aircraft. The story ended:

As long as a year ago there were brief but specific mentions in the Soviet technical press of successful ground testing of atomic aircraft power plants. Recent speculative stories in the Soviet popular press suggest conditioning the Russian people to an announcement of a spectacular achievement by an atomic powered airplane in the near future, probably a non-stop non-fueled flight around the world.

This steady flow of phony "intelligence" came from the missile press, from Congressional sources, from industrial sources, and from the lower levels of the Air Force. General Keirn himself did not specifically claim that he had solid evidence of a Russian program. Rather, in response to a question from Senator Anderson in the hearings referred to earlier, he said only, "I have an intuitive feeling myself that they [the Russians] are quite well along the road." He was then asked (and this was 1959) whether he felt there was any possibility of a Russian nuclear-propelled airplane within two years, and he replied, "I think there is a possibility of it."

President Eisenhower, who, of course, had all intelligence

information available to him, as well as the best possible interpretations of that information, said on December 10, 1958,
"There is absolutely no intelligence to back up a report that
Russia is flight-testing an atomic-powered plane." Today it is
quite obvious that no such nuclear aircraft ever existed in the
Soviet Union and that stories to that effect were simply one
more very clear and very obvious loose attempt to generate
what may be called self-serving intelligence, something which
can be found again and again in other debates over weapons
systems. At the time, the true nature of this "intelligence" was
not at all obvious, even to fairly well-informed people, and
those of us who had all the facts in the matter and who knew
there was no real basis for any of these claims were hamstrung
in any attempts we made to deal with them by the secrecy
which always surrounds real intelligence information. I do not
mean by any of the foregoing that intelligence-type information was deliberately or maliciously falsified. Indeed, if that
had been the case, the Administration's problem in dealing
with the matter would have had a simple solution: expose the
falsifiers. Rather, what happened was that isolated facts and
rumors were assembled, and then analyzed and interpreted by
zealous amateurs until the result was almost pure wishful
thinking and self-delusion. And since the recipients of these
phony intelligence analyses were very frequently as eager and
as predisposed to believe them as were their purveyors, it was
extremely difficult to deal effectively with them.

The story of the ANP, it seems to me, provides a classic il-
lustration of some of the forces that drive the arms race on-
ward. It involves partisan politics: Congress was controlled
by the Democrats, the White House by the Republicans. It
provides a classic example of the exploitation of the fears and
anxieties of the public through the use of imaginary "intelligence." It shows how sincere people who badly want to be
misled can easily mislead themselves: the so-called intelligence
that was used as one of the arguments in support of a crash

program by our side was based in part on technical articles which really did appear in the Soviet press about possible uses of atomic energy, including application of nuclear propulsion to aircraft. These articles were strictly theoretical, but it was quite easy for persons who wanted to believe that the Russians were ahead, to believe it with passion. The ANP story shows how an industrial organization, in this case General Electric, does not merely do what the government asks it to do, but rather works very hard through all possible channels to make sure that the government asks it to do what it wants to do in the first place. It shows how military advocates of programs, especially programs involving more than one agency, attempt to take advantage of all the internal rivalries and tensions which exist in order to find a successful path for the accomplishment of what they—very sincerely, to be sure—believe to be essential, and which they therefore believe justifies the use of any tactics to ensure that administrators will not be able "to put the budget ahead of survival."

5

ROCKETS AND MISSILES

There are a staggering variety of missiles in the world today. They come in a great range of sizes; they exhibit many forms and shapes, and they are designed to accomplish a wide variety of specific objectives. Some missiles are nothing more than pilotless aircraft. Their weight is supported on wings, and they are propelled by jet engines which burn common liquid fuels such as kerosene and gasoline. Missiles of this type are usually known as "cruise missiles" or "air-breathing missiles." Other missiles are shaped more like elongated bullets and are rapidly accelerated to high velocities by rocket motors. Then, like a bullet, they coast along a trajectory determined by their initial momentum and the force of gravity acting on them. Missiles of this type are called "ballistic missiles."

Some missiles are designed to be used for strategic warfare; i.e., their purpose is to eliminate the basic war-making potential of any enemy by killing his people and destroying his factories. Other missiles are designed to be used tactically: their purpose is to destroy enemy soldiers and weapons in direct combat circumstances. Still other missiles are designed to be used for defense: their purpose is to intercept and destroy attacking aircraft and missiles.

The rockets which launch manned and unmanned satellites into orbit around the earth or onto a trajectory to the moon are, of course, technologically identical with those which are used to launch ballistic missiles on their paths toward an enemy target. The only really important difference between the two is in the cargo. Thus it is not surprising that the technological and political histories of the space program and the missile program are tightly interwoven.

The only strategic missiles that have ever been fired in anger in modern times were the German V-1 and V-2. In the waning days of World War II these missiles were used to bombard London and various seaports in Allied hands, both in England and on the Continent.

The V-1 was a winged air-breathing cruise missile propelled by a pulse jet engine. It weighed just under five thousand pounds; its fuselage was twenty-seven feet long and thirty-three inches in diameter. It carried a one-ton chemical-explosive payload. Its rudimentary control system was preset for the range and direction of its target before takeoff, and as a consequence its accuracy was very poor. It was also quite unreliable and highly vulnerable to defensive measures. Considerably less than half of the eight thousand V-1s (or buzz bombs, as the English called them) launched toward London actually arrived there; the majority were either intercepted by British air defenses or went completely astray.

The V-2 was a ballistic missile propelled by a rocket motor using alcohol as its fuel and liquid oxygen as its oxidizer. (Rockets normally carry with them both of the chemical components necessary for the combustion: a fuel and an oxidizer. Jet-type missile engines, of course, get the oxygen they need for combustion directly from the air, as do airplane and automobile engines.) The V-2 was forty-six feet long and sixty-five inches in diameter, and it weighed 27,000 pounds. Just as the fuel was exhausted (or "at burnout," as it is usually called) the missile reached a speed of very nearly one mile per second. As a direct consequence of this speed its maximum range was approximately two hundred miles. At the time, it was the fastest vehicle that had ever been built, and it was not much slower than even today's satellite launchers and intercontinental ballistic missiles, which reach speeds in the neighborhood of five miles per second. The V-2 was steered to its target by what is called an "inertial guidance system." That means that it carried within itself a mechanism which could (1) sense how fast and in what direction it was moving and (2), based on that information, give orders to the propulsion and flight-control systems to make it arrive at a predetermined destination. The accuracy of this guidance system was such that most of the missiles landed within three to five miles of the target selected, or, to put it differently, within a distance from the target which was about two percent of the range to the target. The V-2's payload of chemical explosive was, like the V-1's, just about one ton in weight. However, entirely unlike the V-1, none of the V-2s were intercepted by British air defenses; 1,500 of them landed in England and killed more than 2,500 persons in all.

Both the V-1 and the V-2 were developed during World War II at Peenemünde, Germany, in a laboratory under the direction of General Walter Dornberger and Wernher von Braun. After the war most of the key personnel, including both Dornberger and Von Braun, plus much equipment and much documentation, were brought to the United States as part of Operation Paper Clip. Some of the persons and equipment ended up in Russian hands, and a few individuals ended up in France and Britain. Much, but by no means all, of the development which followed in the U.S.A. and the U.S.S.R. was based on the German experience and involved the participation of these former members of the Peenemünde team.

During the war none of the Allied powers carried on any program aimed at the development of large strategic missiles in the V-1 or V-2 class, but they all did develop and manufacture smaller missiles and rockets for other purposes. One of the best-known of these is, of course, the hand-held bazooka.

One of the most important, insofar as its long-range consequences were concerned, was the JATO (jet-assisted takeoff)
rocket used to assist slow, heavy aircraft (such as seaplanes)
in taking off.

In the United States there were several different projects for
developing and producing these JATO rockets. One of these,
supported by the Navy, was under the direction of Robert H.
Goddard, the "father" of rocketry in this country. Others were
conducted by Reaction Motors, Inc. (originally formed by
members of the American Rocket Society), by GALCIT
(Guggenheim Aeronautical Laboratory, California Institute of
Technology) and the Aerojet General Corporation. Some of
these wartime JATO units developed thrusts in the neighborhood of three thousand pounds.

Two entirely different types of rocket motors were used for
these JATO applicators; one kind used liquid propellants and
the other kind used solid propellants.

In the case of liquid-propellant engines, such as propelled
the V-2, two liquids, one a fuel and the other an oxidizer, are
pumped into a combustion chamber. There they mix and burn,
producing high temperatures and high pressures which force
their combustion products to exhaust through a nozzle in the
tail of the rocket with great speed. In the process of exhausting
to the rear they cause the rocket to recoil in the opposite direction, thus driving it forward. The most practical of the various
fuels used during the war was aniline, and the usual oxidizer
was red fuming nitric acid. Both of these liquids are nasty to
handle, but they have the advantage of being storable at room
temperature (unlike liquid oxygen) and of igniting on contact,
so that no special ignition system is needed to get things started
(unlike the case when kerosene is used as the fuel).

The solid-propellant motors are more like those used in
Fourth of July rockets: the fuel and the oxidizer are already
mixed in a dry form, and then are lighted at one end. A narrow
burning zone rapidly moves through the mixture, creating high-

temperature, high-pressure gaseous combustion products as it does so. These, as in the case of the liquid rocket, exhaust rearward through a nozzle, causing the rocket as a whole to recoil and thus move forward in the process. A mixture commonly used in World War II consisted of asphalt (which acted both as the fuel and as the binder holding the mixture together) plus potassium perchlorate, a powerful oxidizer in the form of a crystalline powder.

The reason the Allies did not attempt to develop missiles for strategic bombardment was a very simple one. With our technological industrial base and with the state of the art as it existed at the time, aircraft were far superior to missiles for such purposes. Aircraft were far more flexible, they could carry much larger payloads, they had much longer ranges, and they could deliver their bombs with much greater accuracy. The V-1 and V-2 missiles were really just psychological terror weapons with very limited direct effectiveness, whereas bombardment aircraft could, in principle at least, go after specific targets such as particular factories, bridges, railroad yards, etc. Also, by the time the Germans began to use the V-weapons, the war was already going very badly for them, and these weapons may have had certain special advantages in just such a situation. For example, the V-2 could be launched from small, easily concealed pads rather than from large, easy-to-see, easy-to-disrupt airfields, and a single missile could get through; whereas the Germans at that time could no longer put up enough aircraft to gain the necessary advantage of saturation.

With the invention and demonstration of nuclear weapons at the close of the war, the whole technological picture changed. The destruction radius of even the earliest nuclear weapons against people, houses, and factories was one or two miles instead of only a hundred feet or so as in the case of even the very largest chemical bombs. This large increase in destruction radius, combined with foreseeable improvements in the accuracy of guided missiles, led weapons-systems designers to give serious consideration to the possibility of producing a new kind of weapon system: the nuclear-armed, intercontinental guided missile. It has become clear such weapons could perform at least some of the functions of bombers.

In the United States, strategic warfare was largely the responsibility of the Army Air Corps (soon to become the U. S. Air Force). Hesitantly at first, it began to explore this new possibility. Both air-breathing cruise missiles and ballistic missiles received serious attention as candidate systems.

Three air-breathing strategic missiles eventually came out of these studies. The first of these was the Snark, a subsonic, winged cruise missile with a range of five thousand to seven thousand miles. Northrup had the prime contract for the development of this missile, and Pratt and Whitney made the jet engines. It was boosted up to operational speed by two large JATO rockets. These were the solid-propellant type and generated a thrust of 33,000 pounds each. The vehicle had a gross weight of fifty thousand pounds and it could carry a payload of five thousand pounds, easily enough for the A-bombs of that day. After a long-drawn-out program, the Snark finally became operational in 1958; it was phased out only a few years later. We realized, several years before Snark became operational, that it would become obsolete by the time it was finally deployed, and repeated recommendations for dropping the project were made. However, in this case as in so many others, the momentum of the project and the politics which surrounded it made it impossible to do so.

The second of the strategic cruise missiles was Matador, for practical purposes a scaled-down Snark. It was built by the Glenn L. Martin Company; it had a gross weight of twelve thousand pounds and a range of 650 miles. It too carried a nuclear warhead. In order to be able to strike at our potential enemies, it had to be based in forward areas such as Japan and Germany. It became operational in 1955 and in the early sixties was replaced by the Mace missile, which had a longer range, greater speed, and superior accuracy.

The third of these large air-breathing winged cruise missiles was the Navaho. This missile was developed by North American Aviation under an Air Force contract. It was started much later than the first two, and consequently its design was based on a much more advanced technology. It was ninety-five feet long, it had small delta wings, and it weighed 300,000 pounds at takeoff. It was boosted into the air and accelerated up to three times the speed of sound (or about two thousand miles per hour) by three large liquid-propellant rocket engines, each one generating 135,000 pounds of thrust. After it reached that speed, ram jets took over and continued to propel it to its target a quarter or more of the way around the world. It was guided by a self-contained all-inertial guidance system. Navaho was flown for the first time in November, 1956, by which time the huge intensive programs to develop intercontinental ballistic missiles were already well under way. It was therefore again recognized, as in the case of Snark, that this weapon system would become obsolete before it was deployed. This time the fact that Navaho was less far along the road toward deployment made it possible to heed the repeated recommendations to cancel the program, and the missile was scrubbed well before it reached operational status.

Even though the Navaho was never deployed, it did play a very important role in our missile program. Its development provided the technological base for much of what was to follow. The large liquid-propellant rocket engines were the first of a long series of similar engines designed and built by Rocketdyne. Later engines in this series powered the Thor, Jupiter, and Atlas missiles and the huge rocket that started Apollo 11 on its journey to the moon more than a decade later. Also, the Navaho inertial-guidance system provided the technological basis of later, more advanced systems which were used in other missiles, aircraft, and even submarines.

In addition to these cruise-type missiles, the Air Force explored the possibility of using large rocket-powered ballistic missiles as intercontinental strategic weapons. In 1946 Consolidated-Vultee (later Convair) was given a contract to look into the matter further, and it began the design and development of the MX-774, an early version of what later became known as the Atlas. Soon after this work was started, and as a result of further internal reviews, the Air Force concluded that, given the existing state of the art, such a weapons system, even with a nuclear warhead, would take too long to develop and would not be competitive with other alternative approaches. The Air Force thereupon decided to discontinue any support for large long-range rockets and to concentrate its resources and energies in the more straightforward and conservative aircraft and cruise-missile programs. Consolidated-Vultee did manage to keep the program going along for a time on its own funds, but for all practical purposes the big-rocket approach to strategic weaponry was dead for the time being in the United States.

During the postwar years the Navy also conducted programs in the development of missiles for a variety of applications. These included the Rigel and then the Regulus I and the Regulus II cruise missiles which could be launched from surfaced submarines and used against either strategic or tactical targets hundreds of miles away on shore. The Navy, like the Air Force, also developed a number of air defense missiles, most of which were rocket-powered. The Army too had a vigorous program of rocket and missile development immediately after World War II. Some of these rockets were developed for the purpose of upper-air research. Other surface-to-surface rockets, including the Corporal, were intended for use in tactical warfare. And still others, including the Nike series, were intended to be used for air defense.

In 1949, the Army decided to establish its major missile-development activities at the Redstone Arsenal in Huntsville, Alabama. Among those transferred were 130 members of the original Von Braun team, as well as many military personnel and other government and contractor employees. The Korean

War broke out soon after this new missile-development group was established. As one result of this new stimulus to weapons development, the Redstone group was given the assignment to develop a longer-range ballistic missile for use in tactical warfare. After a brief period of some uncertainty, it was eventually established that this rocket should have a range of two hundred miles and carry a nuclear warhead. It was to be a mobile weapon capable of being launched under battlefield conditions by regular combat troops. The missile finally designed to meet these objectives was named the Redstone after the Arsenal. It was propelled by a slightly modified version of the 135,000-pound liquid-propellant rocket engine which was being developed by the Rocketdyne Division of North American Aviation for the Air Force's Navaho missile. The Redstone was the largest American rocket under development in the early fifties and, as we shall see, was to form the base for much of the program which followed. As a weapon, however, it never served any important function, and it was often referred to by other Army personnel as "the world's most expensive roadblock."

Starting in the fall of 1952, a series of closely spaced events wrought revolutionary changes in the content and style of our missile-development programs and, through them, all other military development programs as well. These were the invention and demonstration of the hydrogen bomb, the election of Eisenhower and the concomitant extensive personnel changes throughout the executive branch (the first complete change in twenty years), and the growing accumulation of intelligence reports which first indicated and then confirmed that the Soviet Union had already launched a major program for the development of large long-range rockets.

Six crash programs to develop long-range nuclear-tipped strategic missiles were born out of the confluence of these three events. These programs dominated the technological scene in this country throughout the fifties. The names of these missiles all became well-known: Atlas, Titan, Minuteman, Thor, Jupiter, and Polaris. The first three are ICBMs (intercontinental ballistic missiles), the next two are IRBMs (intermediate-range ballistic missiles), and the last is an SLBM (sea- or submarine-launched ballistic missile). All six programs were started within three years of each other, and for a time all six were being carried out concurrently. All six missiles had the same principal purpose: massive retaliation in the event of an attack. In retrospect it is clear that three such programs would have been entirely sufficient, and it would not have been necessary to have even these three all conducted on a crash basis. Why, then, did we overreact? The reason, once again, was the inflation of the anticipated threat and the multiplication of programs designed to counter it—in short, excessive caution and prudence inspired by the thought which is the motto of the arms race: "Let us err on the side of military safety." In addition, the personal ambition of clever men played an essential role in at least one case.

Among the new officials who came into office as a result of Eisenhower's election were Donald A. Quarles, the new Assistant Secretary of Defense for Research and Development (and soon after Secretary of the Air Force), and Trevor Gardner, whose title was Special Assistant to the Secretary of the Air Force. Quarles had been president of the Sandia Corporation, where the final engineering of nuclear weapons is done; he was intelligent, conservative, cautious, and unflappable. Gardner was intelligent, vigorous, somewhat volatile, and impatient to make changes quickly.

Each of these two men in his own style was responsible for first initiating and then guiding the thoroughgoing reviews of the defense research and development program that soon followed the change in administration. The reviews themselves were carried out at first by a number of committees working separately in each of the military services and reporting to different levels of program management. These committees had a strongly interlocking membership, a feature of the advisory apparatus which then, as now, allowed information to travel both up and down within agencies and laterally between agencies and thus to pass over and around the various barriers of secrecy, propriety, and bureaucracy which would otherwise cripple technical progress. (This style of organization and operation, of course, also allows a few strong-minded individuals to dominate a broad part of the scene.)

After about a year, in the interest of making more rapid progress and more profound changes, the originally large number of committees were regrouped into a much smaller number and John von Neumann became the chairman of the most important of them. The "Von Neumann Committee" (under different formal names) advised the Secretary of the Air Force on the projects that were under the direct control of that service, and it advised the Secretary of Defense on all large military rocket programs, including those of the Army and the Navy. Von Neumann was extremely intelligent, and curious about everything. He looked like a cherub and sometimes acted like one; my three- and five-year-old daughters delighted in climbing on him when he came to call at the house. He was very powerful and productive in pure science and mathematics and at the same time had a remarkably strong streak of practicality. He was one of the earliest pioneers in the design and construction of large electronic computers, he developed a strong interest in the technology of nuclear and other weapons, and he made a number of elegant inventions in each of these fields. This combination of scientific ability and practicality gave him a credibility with military officers, engineers, industrialists, and scientists that no one else could match. He was the clearly dominant advisory figure in nuclear missilery at the time, and everyone took his statements about what could and should be done very seriously. Other key members of his committee were George Kistiakowsky and Jerome Wiesner (both of whom later became Special Assistants to Presidents of the United States), Simon Ramo and Dean Wooldridge (both of whom soon left the committee to organize the Ramo-Wooldridge Corporation), and Charles A. Lindbergh. Darol Froman, from the Los Alamos Scientific Laboratory, and I, from the Livermore Laboratory, were also members and in an informal sense represented the nuclear-weapons laboratories. The committee also maintained very close working relationships with the key experts in other essential subfields of technology. Especially important among these was Stark Draper, the director of the Instrument Laboratory at M.I.T. Draper knows more by far about the science and technology of inertial-guidance systems than anyone else in the Western world. He is a great optimist, and, although he is usually right, he sometimes seems to know even more than is so.

Working very closely with Gardner, Quarles, and Air Force Generals James McCormack and Bernard A. Schriever, the Von Neumann Committee in a series of intensive meetings in 1953 and early 1954 concluded that:

1. The state of the art in the relevant branches of technology had reached the point where a practical rocket-powered ballistic missile capable of carrying a nuclear warhead intercontinental distances and delivering it with sufficient accuracy could be built.

2. The Soviets had a head start of some years in this field, and therefore the United States should initiate a program with the "highest national priority" to build such a missile (the Atlas).

3. A new style of program management and technical direction was needed to coordinate properly the disparate fields of technology involved and to conduct concurrently the development, production, and deployment phases of the program.

In response to this third recommendation the Air Force established the Western Development Division (WDD) of the Air Research and Development Command (ARDC), selected then Brigadier General Schriever to command it, and gave him an unusual combination of authorities over the research, development, and procurement phases of the program. Schriever used his special authority brilliantly, and much of what we now take for granted in the methodology of systems development and systems management was pioneered under his direction. He was able to integrate a wide variety of persons and facilities effectively and with finesse. In contrast to that of the more typical project officer, his personal influence made a real and positive difference to the program. In addition, and at least as important, the Air Force gave a contract to the then spanking-new Ramo-Wooldridge Corporation to provide what the weapons trade now refers to as general systems engineering and technical direction, or, more commonly, GSETD. At first this contract covered only the Atlas ICBM, but it later was extended to include all of the large Air Force ballistic missiles. The Ramo-Wooldridge organization supplied the scientific and technical expertise needed to complement and supplement the expertise in program administration and military matters which Schriever had directly on his staff. Ramo and Wooldridge assembled with remarkable speed a very strong group of scientists and engineers and did another excellent job.

Ramo and Wooldridge themselves had been members of the earlier versions of the Von Neumann Committee, and it was no coincidence that their new corporation was given this GSETD assignment as its very first job. There was absolutely nothing improper or wrong about this arrangement, but it does indicate that the "arm's-length" relationship between government and business which is generally thought of as being part of the free-enterprise system was even then missing from what years later came to be known as the "military-industrial complex." The Ramo-Wooldridge Corporation at first was strictly limited to planning and technical management and was prohibited from working on any hardware development or production. However, the corporation later merged with Thompson Products (which always had been in hardware) and now operates as a major, well-known general defense contractor under the name TRW, Inc. One of its subsidiaries, TRW Systems, still performs general systems engineering and technical direction under contract to the Air Force on the Minuteman ICBM, one of the later missile programs which I will discuss shortly. (In 1960, a new, nonprofit corporation, the Aerospace Corporation, was established to provide GSETD for most Air Force missile and space programs. Many of the key personnel, including the senior vice-president technical, Allen Donovan, transferred from TRW to the new corporation in order to assure the smoothest possible transition.)

History can't be run by twice in order to check out alternatives, but I believe that without either WDD and General Schriever or the Ramo-Wooldridge group, the Atlas project would have taken more than a year longer to complete and would have cost much more as a consequence.

After the decision to go ahead with the development of large long-range rockets, or ICBMs, and after this new organizasional structure came into being, the Von Neumann Committee, then working very closely with both WDD and the Ramo-Wooldridge Corporation, focused its attention on the technical details of the system. By an iterative process, the committee established both the performance goals (or "specs") and a first rough outline of a design which would meet them.

The performance goals set for the Atlas, the first ICBM to be started, were the following: a one-megaton-warhead explosive yield, 5,500 nautical miles range, and five miles or better accuracy, or CEP ("circular error probable," the distance from the target within which, on the average, half of the warheads fall). The accuracy specified for this missile thus called for the warheads to land within a distance *from* the target which was only one tenth of one percent of the range *to* the target. In this sense, the accuracy required was twenty times that actually achieved by the V-2 ten years earlier. I emphasize this matter of accuracy because steady improvements in it have had a more profound effect on the arms race than any other technological factor, save only the invention of the H-bomb.

It is most instructive to examine the origin of these numbers. Draper, always a technical optimist, said he could foresee much better CEPs than five miles, and we simply took that figure as a conservative estimate. The range figure of 5,500 nautical miles is not, as one might suppose, the distance between two given points, one in the U.S.A. and one in the U.S.S.R. (Such distances vary from five miles to eight thousand miles or so.) Rather, it is precisely one fourth of the earth's circumference. It was, however, a sensible figure to focus on, being easily typical of heartland-to-heartland distances. Further, at a range of 5,500 miles the range of a rocket depends very strongly on its initial speed, so only small fractional changes in this latter quantity enable the range to be varied from, say, 3,500 miles to eight thousand miles.

The origin of the remaining performance goal, the requirement of a one-megaton yield, is much more interesting to examine. It is true that the damage radius of a one-megaton bomb is more or less compatible with the accuracy prescribed for the missile. However, the accuracy goal itself was arbitrary; the definition of damage is quite imprecise, and the radius at which a given blast pressure is generated varies only very slowly with the yield (as the cube root, in fact). Thus, the damage radius of a ten-megaton bomb and a one-hundred-kiloton bomb could equally well be said to be compatible with the prescribed accuracy. So, why 1.0 megaton? The answer is because and only because one million is a particularly round number in our culture. We picked a one-megaton yield for the Atlas warhead for the same reason that everyone speaks of rich men as being millionaires and never as being tenmillionaires or one-hundred-thousandaires. It really was that mystical, and I was one of the mystics. Thus, the actual physical size of the first Atlas warhead and the number of people it would kill were determined by the fact that human beings have two hands with five fingers each and therefore count by tens.

What if we had had six fingers on each hand and therefore counted by twelves instead of tens? As any school child who takes modern math knows, the number one-million in base twelve is fully three times as big as the number one-million in base ten. Thus, if evolution had given us six fingers on each hand, our first ICBM warhead would have had to be three times as big, the rockets to deliver them would have threatened the lives of up to three times as many human beings, and it would have taken one or two years longer to carry out their development program. Similarly, if we had had only four fingers, like some comic-strip characters, the first warheads and missiles would have been only one-fourth as large, we could have built them somewhat sooner, and the present overkill problem would not be nearly as serious as it is. The only funny thing about this story is that it is true. It really was that arbitrary, and, what's more, that same arbitrariness has stayed with us. The initiation of other, later missile programs, including the Minuteman and the Polaris, was in fact delayed until nuclear-weapons technology advanced to the point where a one-megaton warhead could be forecast for each of them too. To go further, but still to remain within the realm of the truly possible, there might never have been a large liquid-fueled Atlas at all if we had had four fingers and hence a base-eight number system. We might have gone directly to the smaller and simpler solid-propellant Minuteman, which eventually did replace the liquid missiles.

Since these performance goals were set, rationalizations for them have been worked out, and many people, including especially those in the military services, think that the yield and all the other numbers characterizing the system can be derived from complex mathematical formulae connecting explosive yield, damage radius, target vulnerability, and other numerically defined quantities.

This particular case of arbitrariness I have been discussing is by no means unique. Defense planning is full of arbitrary figures and figurings that have been thoroughly rationalized only after the fact. The number of units of many types of equipment is almost as arbitrary; so are the total numbers of men in the various services; and hence so is the total defense budget itself. I would say that the defense budget is arbitrary by at least a factor of two. The fierce arguments that can break out over a cut of, say, five percent have their origins in the very great difficulties of making changes in large traditionbound systems and not in the fact that the numbers as they originally stood were correct in any absolute sense. Thus, the real reason that this year's defense budget is so and so many billion dollars is simply that last year's defense budget was so and so many billion, give or take about five percent. The same thing, of course, applies to last year's budget and the budget of the year before that. Thus the defense budget is not what it is for any absolute reason or because in any absolute sense the total cost of everything that is supposedly truly needed comes out to be precisely that amount, but rather it is the sum total of all the political influences that have been applied to it over a history of many years, and that have caused it to grow in the way that it has grown. (The foregoing, of course, excludes special events like the Vietnam War, but even at its height that conflict has absorbed considerably less than half of the defense dollars.)

A similar situation also prevails with respect to over-all manpower needs. I became convinced when I was in the Pentagon later in the "missile gap" days that the apparent approximately ten percent shortage of technical personnel had nothing to do with the fact that there was a real need for an absolute number of persons which happened by a remarkable coincidence to be just ten percent more than we then had. Rather, the number of technical people then working could generate and sell ideas that needed ten percent more people to accomplish them. If there had been twice as many scientists and engineers in our defense programs, there would still have been about a ten percent shortage, and if there had been half as many, the shortage we would have seen would even so have been only about ten percent.

Getting back to the Atlas story, after setting the performance goals, the Von Neumann Committee, Ramo-Wooldridge, and the Western Development Division were then able to outline the basic design of the system. The committee first estimated that the "required" one-megaton explosion could be produced by a nuclear weapon which, together with the protective reentry nose cone, would weigh 3,500 pounds. (A year previously, an Air Force Science Advisory Board panel, also chaired by John von Neumann, and including Teller and me as members, had predicted that a warhead of that weight would soon become feasible.) With the fuels then available, and for a given design style, immutable laws of physics connected the payload weight with the total rocket gross weight, and this was determined to be in the neighborhood of 250,000 pounds. With this as a base, it could then be decided that two large booster engines plus one smaller sustainer engine could accomplish the task of propelling the missile. The booster engine selected was the large liquid-powered Navaho engine uprated to 150,000 pounds of thrust each, and the sustainer engine was to be of similar design but reduced in size and generating only sixty thousand pounds thrust. It was further determined that the guidance and control equipment should be of the inertial type but assisted by radar observations of the rocket made from the ground during the takeoff. Such observations helped to further refine the ability of the missile to know where it was, how fast it was going, and where it was headed. The airframe, most of which consisted of the tanks containing the propellants, was to be made of very thin steel so that it would be light enough to enable the rocket to reach the high velocity necessary for an intercontinental range. In fact, the airframe had to be so lightly constructed that it could not stand up on its own. It had to be continuously internally pressurized like a large balloon in order to hold its own weight plus the warhead and the other equipment placed up forward. In over-all dimensions, the Atlas was over eighty feet long and ten feet in diameter and weighed about a quarter of a million pounds.

Under the general technical direction of Ramo-Wooldridge, Convair (later called General Dynamics/Astronautics) was the contractor selected to build the airframe and to manage the over-all assembly of the missile, Rocketdyne Division of North American Aviation was given the propulsion contract, General Electric/Syracuse was given the contract for the inertial-guidance and control subsystem, General Electric/Philadelphia was given the contract for the reentry nose cone, and Los Alamos was assigned the job of designing the nuclear warhead. I must note here with some personal chagrin that, while it had been the Livermore Laboratory that was brash enough to promise that a one-megaton warhead could be made in a small enough physical package, it was the Los Alamos Scientific Laboratory that was mature enough at the time to actually provide one.

The task of developing materials and shapes suitable for the reentry nose cone, so that it could withstand the extreme conditions encountered at reentry, was often held up as the most difficult of all the problems associated with ICBMs. The public press, including the news magazines, was full of vivid stories comparing the reentering missile warhead to a meteor. I felt then that this was a grossly overestimated problem. As it finally turned out, it was necessary to approach this problem with some care, but a number of quite different but adequate solutions were discovered. As a direct result of the exaggerated views of the difficulty of this problem, much more money was spent on this aspect of the program than was really necessary.

The Atlas program was very successful in most respects. It exceeded most of its performance goals, and it met the schedule laid down at the very beginning of the program. First flight with all three engines going was in August, 1958, and resulted in a range of about 2,500 miles. By 1960 an Atlas launched out over the Atlantic reached a range of nine thousand miles, and in that same year the first units became operational. However, over-all reliability from countdown to launch to flight was never good, especially for the operational units. Perhaps only as few as twenty percent of them would have reached their targets in a real war situation during the first year or so of so-called operational readiness.

In 1955, immediately after the Atlas program was under way and had been given the "highest national priority," two additional missile programs were initiated by the Air Force. The responsibility for the development of the Thor and the Titan, as they were called, was placed under the same management combination, and both programs were given the very same "highest national priority."

The range goal of the Thor was set at only 1,500 miles, but its other performance goals were left to be the same as Atlas. To meet these goals it needed only one engine instead of three, its tankage could be constructed with heavier walls so that it could stand without internal pressurization, and its top speed would be enough slower so that the reentry problem would also be much simpler. It was to be a "technical fallout" of the Atlas program and therefore was to use Atlas components to the maximum extent possible. The Thor program was quite successful from a strictly technical point of view. In addition to being briefly deployed as a strategic weapon, Thors have been used as the main booster stage for launching a great many satellites into orbit.

Along with the fact that Thor was a simple, direct and therefore hopefully inexpensive "technical fallout" from the Atlas program, there were two other rationalizations given for building it. The first of these, which made considerable sense in the context of the time, was that we thought it could be deployed one or two years sooner than the Atlas, and therefore we could perhaps eliminate some or all of the time advantage the Russians had because of their earlier start. Of course, since these missiles did not have a truly intercontinental range, it would be necessary to deploy them overseas close to the Soviet Union. However, with our worldwide system of alliances, that did not appear to be a serious problem, and in 1960 they were deployed in the United Kingdom. A second rationalization put forward by a number of influential persons at the time was simply that since the Russians were believed to be working on an intermediate-range ballistic missile (IRBM), we must have one, too. It turned out be correct that the Russians were working on an IRBM of their own, and they now do have a great many of them deployed within the Soviet Union. However, the Soviet situation and the American situation are by no means symmetrical insofar as the need for missiles in this range is concerned. The Soviet Union has a great many potential enemies within 1,500 miles of its borders, whereas at the time the United States had no enemies that near its borders. Furthermore, the United States had a great deal of war materiel in the form of tactical aircraft and many other kinds of equipment deployed within 1,500 miles of the Soviet Union, whereas the Soviet Union had no equipment of any kind deployed that near the United States. There was, therefore, no symmetry whatsoever as far as the possible need for such a weapon was concerned, and this argument really had no more intellectual content than the familiar household notion about keeping up with the Joneses no matter what they do.

Also in early 1955, the Air Force initiated the development of a third large liquid-fueled rocket, the Titan. Its performance goals were the same as those of the Atlas, and its over-all dimensions were very nearly the same, but its design differed in a fundamental way. In contrast to Atlas, Titan employed a straightforward two-stage design. In such a design, the first, or booster, stage accelerates the missile up to about half of the final velocity needed to reach the target. Then, with the first-stage propellants exhausted, the engines and the tankage of the first stage drop off. At that point the second-stage engine starts up and the payload is accelerated on up to full velocity. This is the style of design used for all long-range rockets except the Atlas and allows a number of simplifications over the Atlas design. The Atlas employed a modified single-stage design in which the two large booster engines were dropped off part way along but the main propellant tanks were carried along the whole way. As a result, the airframe, which consisted very largely of the propellant tankage, had to be so lightly constructed that it could not stand up on its own. It had to be pressurized internally like a large steel balloon to support its own weight plus the weight of the payload. In the case of the Titan, and of all true multistage rockets, it is possible to use heavier construction for the tankage and hence it is not necessary to rely on internal pressurization to supply the needed rigidity and strength.

We had realized when we started the Atlas back in 1954 that the Titan design was the ideal one, but we had avoided it because it required that the second-stage engine be started at altitude. At that time, there was practically no experience with starting liquid-rocket engines under such conditions—i.e., in a vacuum and perhaps in a state of free fall. The Atlas design, awkward as it otherwise was, allowed all engines to be started on the ground before launch, so at the time it seemed prudent to use it for the first approach. We anticipated even then that we would later start another program parallel to Atlas. The Titan project brought in a complete new set of contractors for all subsystems and therefore provided a backup not only for the Atlas as a whole, but, indeed, for any part of it. As it turned out, the altitude-start problem gave us no difficulty at all, and the development of Titan proceeded reasonably smoothly. The first Titan was placed in service in 1962, less than two years after the first Atlas. Eventually a later, much improved and somewhat larger version of Titan replaced both the Atlases and the first Titans in our operational inventory. In retrospect, it is clear that our approach to ICBM design was unnecessarily conservative in the way it treated unknowns such as reentry and engine starts at altitude. If we had started with the Titan design in the first place in 1954, we could have done a somewhat better job on about the same time schedule. Such an approach would have cost much less, since no second large liquid-propellant rocket system would have been needed.

In 1957, the Air Force also started yet another ICBM development program, this time based on the use of solid propellants rather than liquid propellants as had been the case with the Atlas, Thor, and Titan. This new missile, called the Minuteman, eventually became the most widely deployed of all and, through the last half of the sixties, provided the main component of our strategic forces.

It had long been held that for most military purposes solid rockets were potentially superior to liquid rockets. They promised greater reliability, readiness, and ease of handling, but their relatively poorer performance in terms of net payload weight for a given total missile weight had prevented their use in long-range ICBM applications. However, by 1957, improvements in this performance factor, coupled with further reductions in the weight of one-megaton thermonuclear weapons, made this use appear to be feasible, and the Minuteman program was accordingly initiated. Even with these advances, three stages were required in order to achieve intercontinental range. The project was considered at first to be marginal, but it eventually worked out very well indeed. A Minuteman flew out of an operational underground silo in late 1961, and about year end 1962 the first Minutemen were deployed. The original version of Minuteman was approximately fifty-six feet long, had a diameter of six feet at its base, and weighed 65,000 pounds. The weight was actually determined by practical considerations involving the transportation of the fully assembled rocket over the interstate highway system. The explosive yield of its warhead was roughly the magic one megaton. The first model of this missile had a less than adequate range, but eventually the range was increased to about 6,500 miles.

The improvement in rocket performance that made inter-continental-range solid rockets feasible did not come from any so-called breakthrough in fuel performance; rather, it came from advances in the much more mundane technology of rocket-case design. In the early fifties and before, the cases containing the mixtures of solid rocket fuels had weights equal to twenty percent and more of the weight of the fuels them-selves. Under such circumstances, intercontinental rockets can-not be built without an impractically large number of stages. In the late fifties techniques developed in the fiber-glass indus-try were adapted for making cases that would withstand the high temperatures and pressures of the burning fuels yet had weights equal to only ten percent of the fuels they contained. As is all too often the situation in the American aerospace complex, a great many people and organizations were working on the exotic problem of developing high-performance fuels, and relatively few were working on the much more important but less sexy problem of case design.

During the period in which the Air Force had been develop-ing its missiles, the Army and the Navy had not been inactive. Determined not to stand aside and let the junior service mo-nopolize the most crucial defense efforts of the day, they were quick to advance their own projects.

The Army's entry in the big-rocket derby was the Jupiter missile. The story of the development and the demise of the Jupiter is a textbook example of how personal determination and zeal, combined with interservice rivalry, can fuel the arms race and result in the production and the deployment of need-less weapons and in the needless expenditure of billions of dollars. For all practical purposes, the Jupiter was identical to the Thor. It had the same range, the same-size warhead, the same accuracy and even the same engines. With only minor variations (its diameter was specially selected so that it could pass through Swiss railway tunnels!), it had the same physical dimensions and it was built on the same schedule. It was developed by an Army organization under the command of General John Bruce Medaris and under the technical direction of Wernher von Braun. It was officially started a few months later than the Thor, although the people who promoted it had evidently been thinking about it for quite some time.

It seems clear, from various historical accounts of the origins of the space program, that perhaps the most important driving force behind the Jupiter program was the same as one of the major reasons for the existence of the V-2: Von Braun's abiding interest in space flight. In Germany at the time of the V-2 development, it was not possible to sell large space programs to Hitler's government, but it was possible to sell terror weapons. In the United States in the early fifties, a modest space program had been authorized as part of the U.S. contribution to the International Geophysical Year. The Von Braun group submitted a proposal for launching a satellite as part of the program, but it lost out to a Navy group in what seems to have been a fair competition. It was not possible to sell yet another space program to our government, but it was possible to sell weapons of mass destruction to the military authorities. And, since long-range ballistic missiles are virtually identical with space boosters except for the payload, Von Braun was "practical" and sold these rockets which really had one purpose on the basis of another.

Of course, many rationalizations for the Jupiter program were offered. These included a purported need for a land mobile tactical weapon having a range of fifteen hundred miles and an explosive yield of a megaton, although to my knowledge no neutral study then revealed the need for anything remotely similar. Another rationalization was that this system could serve as a backup to the Thor, although, since the Thor itself was justified principally as a temporary stand-in for the Atlas, it is difficult to see now how this could have been taken very seriously, even in the context of the missile race as we then understood it. A third rationalization was that the Jupiter could serve as an intermediate-range missile to be launched by ships or submarines stationed in the open seas near the Eurasian land mass. The Navy did have, then as now, a role in strategic warfare, and, as a result, a joint Army–Navy group whose purpose was to adapt the Jupiter missile for shipboard and possible submarine use was established in November, 1955. The Navy never really liked this arrangement, since it involved having another service build a missile for its use. (The same thing was seen again years later in the TFX controversy, when Secretary McNamara tried to arrange for the design of a single aircraft suitable for both Air Force and Navy use.) Furthermore, the Navy took a very dim view of the idea of placing large liquid-fueled missiles on board ships and, even worse, on board submarines. These missiles, as then designed, had to be fueled with large amounts of liquid oxygen at the last minute, and the problems associated with this seemed to be extremely difficult.

Therefore, right from the start the Navy was on the lookout for some way out of this arrangement. The steady march of technical progress soon provided it with one. The Livermore Laboratory predicted that the package that would produce a one-megaton explosive yield could be further reduced in size. At the same time, important improvements in the performance characteristic of solid-propellant rockets were being made at Aerojet and other industrial laboratories. A special group under the leadership of Admiral William F. Raborn reviewed these advances and concluded that it had become possible to build what we now call the Polaris system.

The original Polaris was a solid-fueled rocket capable of throwing a new one-megaton warhead a distance of somewhat more than a thousand miles. It was 28.5 feet long and 54

inches in diameter and weighed 28,000 pounds. It was sized
so that sixteen Polaris rockets could be fitted aboard a nuclear-
powered submarine. The potentially nasty problem of handling
liquid fuels, especially liquid oxygen, was completely eliminated. The joint Army–Navy committee was dissolved, and the
Special Project Office, which performed brilliantly under the
leadership of Admiral Raborn and then Captain Levering
Smith, was set up and took over the program, now entirely
within the jurisdiction of the Navy. The Polaris program itself
proceeded very smoothly, and the first Polaris missiles were
deployed at sea aboard the *George Washington* in November
of 1960. In so doing, and despite its late start, the Polaris program became the first of our strategic missile programs to
make a substantial contribution to our strategic power.

Soon after the initiation of the Polaris program, word got
around that Secretary of Defense Charles E. Wilson did not
consider the remaining rationalization sufficient justification
for the existence of two nearly identical liquid-fueled IRBM
programs, and that therefore one of them, probably the Jupiter, which by then had become a backup to a stopgap, would
have to go. Medaris and Von Braun got wind of this potential
calamity in time, and, with Secretary of the Army Wilber M.
Brucker as a more than willing ally, they were able to ward
it off, though not completely. As a result of their efforts, the
Jupiter program was allowed to continue, but the operational
responsibility for all missiles in the intermediate and intercontinental ranges was given to the Air Force. While not a very
desirable solution to the problem from the Army point of
view, this did have the virtue of keeping the program alive a
little longer. The Jupiter was eventually deployed as an IRBM
weapon in Turkey and Italy. There, nestled in the left armpits
of the Russians, so to speak, it probably helped to inspire them
to deploy some of their intermediate-range ballistic missiles
in a similar fashion in a corresponding location, namely, the
island of Cuba.

There was some useful technological fallout from the Jupiter program. This included the successful development and testing of the cheaper ablative type of reentry nose cone, and the development of a quite different rocket system, known as Jupiter C, which was later used to launch the first United States satellites. In addition, it kept the Von Braun team employed during what would otherwise have been some lean years. Even so, it seems to me that justifying the program because of these secondary benefits is like justifying five years' study of Latin so as to more clearly understand the difference between direct and indirect objects of verbs in English. There clearly were better ways of achieving the same objectives.

Altogether, during the fifties, we had initiated six crash programs to develop long-range nuclear strategic missiles. In retrospect, it is clear that three would have been sufficient.

Which of the three would have sufficed? Why did we overreact? What were the conseqences of the overreaction?

A sufficient program would have consisted of the Titan plus the Minuteman plus the Polaris. Excessive technical conservatism led us to build both the Atlas and the Titan. The two offered the same general performance characteristics in terms of payload, range, and accuracy. We knew that the Titan design was intrinsically superior, but, because we had doubts about solving certain problems inherent in it, we started with the less risky Atlas first and did not take up the Titan until about a year later. As it turned out, both worked, but only one was needed. To be sure, hindsight is better than foresight, and probably we did the best we could under the circumstances at the time. But, even so, there is a valuable lesson here to be remembered the next time this sort of problem arises.

I regard both Thor and Jupiter to have been unnecessary. As I related above, the main justification for Thor was that it could serve as a stopgap for some period of time before the more complicated and difficult Atlas ICBM could be deployed. As things turned out, it never did so in any strategically significant sense. The same arguments apply, with greater force, to the Jupiter. Both of these rockets did later serve as booster stages for space-vehicle launchers for a time, but other alternatives were available which would have cost much less in the long run.

As a result, we spent about twice as much money and we employed about twice as many people on these development programs as we should have. Furthermore, from the point of view of military security such excesses were harmful because they caused us to stretch our resources thinner than was really necessary. The early operational versions of these missiles all had a very much lower reliability than was predicted. They were therefore rather ineffective as strategic weapons for the first several years after their deployment began. It is quite likely that if we had been able to concentrate our top talent on fewer programs, this situation would not have been quite as bad. The same thing can be said about other problems and "bugs" that took time to fix. All in all, I believe the three sufficient programs could have been accomplished significantly sooner than they were if they had not had to compete with the three excess programs.

From the point of view of arms control and the arms race, these excesses in dollars and people also had serious consequences. The extra organizations and the extra people resulted in a larger constituency favoring weapons development. This larger constituency in turn strengthened those forces in the Congress "which hear the farthest drum before the cry of a hungry child," and consequently the whole arms race spiraled faster than before. Many of the leaders within this overexpanded missile industry correctly foresaw that they would be in trouble when all of these concurrent crash development programs finally resulted in some deployed hardware. They rightly anticipated that any follow-on developments would have a very hard time competing with the even larger funds needed for such deployments, and they provided some of the most strident voices among those proclaiming the "missile gap" of the 1958–60 period, but that is the subject of a later chapter.

In addition to all these missile programs, there were under way in the United States in the immediate pre-Sputnik era three entirely separate programs whose objectives were orbiting artificial satellites.

One of these was the Vanguard program, under the general supervision of the National Academy of Sciences. Its objective was the orbiting of a small artificial satellite as part of the United States contribution to the IGY, or International Geophysical Year. This rather special year was eighteen months long, extending from mid-1957 through 1958. The Navy, which was assigned the specific responsibility for developing the launch vehicle, was told to make it no bigger than absolutely necessary and to avoid interfering with any military-rocket programs. These two requirements together almost foredoomed it to failure, though it did eventually successfully launch three very small payloads weighing three, twenty-one, and one hundred pounds.

The second U. S. satellite program then under way was under the direction of the Air Force. It was actually a collection of a number of projects with different specific military objectives. In the immediate post-Sputnik days we usually described these as "communications relay," "navigation aids," "weather," "reconnaissance," "early warning," etc. From the first the payloads involved were scheduled to weigh over one thousand pounds, and eventually they in fact weighed many thousands of pounds. They were scheduled for first flight in 1959, when the IGY would be over.

These Air Force satellites were to be launched into space with large rockets consisting of either Thor or Atlas as the first stage plus a special upper stage called Agena. The Agena was built by Lockheed on an Air Force contract let in 1956. It went through a series of modifications during its service as the workhorse of the military space program. On February 28, 1959, a Thor-Agena combination injected a 1,450-pound satellite into orbit.

The third pre-Sputnik satellite program was bootlegged by the Army. The Von Braun group had earlier submitted a proposal for a rocket for launching the IGY satellite to the committee duly charged with launcher selection. In what I understand to have been a fair competition, the winner was the Navy's Vanguard proposal. However, the Medaris–Von Braun group was not one to be stopped by a mere decision of higher authority, and they went ahead and designed a new satellite launcher which they named the Jupiter C. Writing in 1960 about the controversy over this matter, Medaris recalled that, after a successful cancer operation in 1956, he developed "the ultimate conviction that the Lord still had work for me to do or my life would not have been spared."

This Jupiter C was not really a Jupiter; rather, it was a Redstone plus upper stages consisting of clusters of small solid rockets. Its ostensible purpose was testing nose-cone materials for Jupiter, but the actual velocity attained (and not accidentally) was more nearly that of an Atlas, the development of which was the sole responsibility of the Air Force. Even on its very first launch, it carried an additional dummy stage, "filled with sand instead of power," which if properly filled and fired could have been used to send it into orbit well in advance of Sputnik and the IGY. According to Medaris in his book *Countdown for Decision,* it was given the name Jupiter C so that it could benefit from the high priority the real Jupiter had. On January 31, 1958, Jupiter C was used to launch America's first satellite, the Explorer I, weighing just thirty-one pounds, into orbit.

6

SPUTNIK

Of all the symbols in the mythology of terror which has propelled the arms race, Sputnik is the most dramatic. The successful launching of the Soviet satellite was inflated by design and circumstance far out of proportion to its real technological and strategic significance into a specter of menace which haunted America for years. It became the crucial psychological landmark in the course of postwar arms development, affecting almost every facet of defense operations.

In August, 1957, the Russians launched a test ICBM on a trajectory that took it the length of Siberia. The launch was conducted in secret, and thus only small "in" groups both here and in the U.S.S.R. which had been following the Soviet program were immediately aware of it. To such people in this country it was a disturbing event, though not at all a surprise. When it was subsequently announced, its meaning was not immediately clear to the public at large.

Less than two months later, on October 4, 1957, the Russians successfully launched the first artificial satellite into orbit. Sputnik was there for all to see and hear, and its name became a part of the language of all civilized men. A wave of shock and consternation swept the United States and most of the rest of the world. Even the small "in" group that had been following the Soviet missile program as it had been gradually revealed through intelligence-gathering means (such as the U-2) was surprised by the suddenness with which this event followed the first long-range-missile launch. To almost everyone else it was unbelievable that the Russians, "those Asiatics" as Truman had called them, could have beaten the United States in this field of highly sophisticated technology.

Very little was known at that time about the state of Soviet science and technology, and what was known did not adequately prepare us for what had happened. The historic Russian passion for secrecy, greatly enhanced by the paranoia of the Soviet government in Stalin's later years, had completely concealed Soviet progress (as well as lack of progress) from the eyes of the world. Even the results of research in pure science had been only partially and reluctantly made known. Travel to Russia by Western scientists had been virtually prohibited until 1954, when the first post-Stalin thaw began. Visits of Russian scientists to the outside world had been similarly restricted, and even the scientific academies were out of touch with each other. The Russians had often claimed that they had been first with many inventions, but it was "obvious" that these were just idle boasts ("obviously" even in the cases where it was true!). About the only Russian invention Westerners were generally aware of was the two-seater farm tractor, whose main function seemed to be to replace the church social as a place where Red Pioneer boys could meet collective-farm girls. Even true-blue Western Communists did not think of the U.S.S.R. as very progressive in technology. To most of the rest of us, Russia was as mysterious and remote as the other side of the moon and not much more productive when it came to really new ideas or inventions. A common joke of the time said that the Russians could not surreptitiously introduce nuclear bombs in suitcases into the United States, because they had not yet been able to perfect a suitcase. The Russian achievement of a nuclear explosion in 1949 and a thermonuclear device in 1953 should have alerted us, but the circumstances surrounding these events were unclear, and it was soon taken for granted that they had stolen "the secret of the bomb" from us.

True enough, the Korean War had revealed the existence of some good fighter aircraft, and the first small exchanges of scientific visits after the death of Stalin had begun to reveal a scientific program of high quality. But a few swallows don't make a summer, and the general picture of the Soviet Union as a basically backward country had not yet begun to change. Thus everyone was shocked, and the reactions of the sophisticated and the unsophisticated differed only in degree.

Sputnik I had weighed 183 pounds. It was followed on November 3 by Sputnik II, which weighed 1,120 pounds and carried the dog Laika as its passenger. In early December, the United States attempted to orbit a three-pound satellite. This was to have been lofted by the Vanguard rocket mentioned earlier, but that system failed to do so. On January 31, 1958, the United States did succeed in orbiting its first satellite, the Explorer I, using the Juno (Jupiter C) rocket booster. Explorer I weighed thirty-one pounds. The second and third American satellites, both launched in March, weighed 3 pounds and thirty-one pounds respectively. In May, the Russians launched Sputnik III, weighing 2,925 pounds.

These huge differences in weight served to worsen considerably the general consternation that pervaded all levels of American society and government. It was widely felt that the Russians must be on to some secret that had evaded us. The fear grew that all this might have some profound effect on our real national security as well as on our prestige. Feeble attempts by the White House to allay our fears by likening the whole matter to a basketball game in space only made things worse. Nearly everyone saw Sputnik as a problem that must be solved and as a challenge that must be met. This situation soon was christened the "missile gap." This name was as simple and catchy as it was misleading, but the truth was so complex that it could not at the time overcome appearances, not even in the mind of an observer with no special ax to grind. Now that enough years have passed so that passions have cooled and the truth has become clear, it is very worthwhile to examine the whole matter anew in order to learn how misleading appearances can be in this kind of situation.

Rather than just one gap, there were a number of important differences or gaps between the programs and accomplishments of the two great powers. There were both a missile gap and a quite distinct space gap, and each of these gaps in turn included separately a time gap and a weight or payload gap. All of these gaps had their origins in differences in how and when the two programs began.

The largest Soviet rockets were designed for use as intercontinental ballistic missiles (ICBMs) whose purpose was to deliver atomic weapons to targets a quarter of the circumference of the world away. The largest rockets under development in the United States had the same purpose. At the time the over-all size of our rockets was fixed, hydrogen-bomb development in the United States had reached a point such that we could fairly accurately predict the size of the warhead needed to produce a one-megaton explosion and hence we could with some assurance also select the rocket size needed to deliver such a bomb. The Soviet decision with respect to size appears to have been made sometime earlier than we made ours, well before the Russians had any practical experience whatsoever in thermonuclear weaponry. Therefore they had to be very much more conservative in their approach to the size question, and, as a result, they chose to build a rocket weighing about twice as much as ours and having about twice our thrust.

This factor of two worked against us in the first phases of the space race, but ultimately worked in our favor in the missile race.

As we now know, by the time the numbers of deployed ICBMs became a significant factor in the strategic balance between the two superpowers, the United States was well ahead of the U.S.S.R. I believe the greater size of the Russians' first ICBM simply made it so difficult to manufacture and deploy that they decided not to do so immediately. Soon after, they did achieve a missile suitable for mass deployment, but even then it took them most of a decade to make up for lost time and catch up with us. None of this was obvious, unfortunately, from those parts of the space race that the public could see and understand. And even those privy to the details could not then have predicted the Russians' failure to exploit their early lead. The Soviet leaders made things more confusing by deliberately using their genuine early space lead to imply an ICBM threat (nonexistent) against the U. S. even as early as 1958.

Besides this factor of two or so in size of booster, two other matters similarly affected the situation. First, we had deliberately decided against using our largest rockets for launching scientific satellites during the 1957–58 International Geophysical Year. Well before Sputnik we had initiated programs designed to use our largest military rockets for launching military satellites (the names Samos and Midas will be recalled by early space-program watchers), but we had specifically ordered that the scientific IGY satellite program not be allowed to interfere with any of our military programs. Therefore we used the specially designed Vanguard and the bootlegged Jupiter C to launch our first satellites. These were much smaller than our large ICBM boosters, in terms of both booster weight and rocket-engine thrust. The Russians, on the other hand, made no such division between their missile program and their space program, and they used the same very large booster for each. Thus, in the satellite exhibition all the world was watching, they were using their biggest rockets and we were using two of our smaller ones.

But even that isn't the whole story. A satellite booster system ordinarily consists of two or three stages. The performance and sizes of these various stages must be carefully matched to each other in order to optimize the payload. In an optimal situation, the commonly used liquid-fuel rockets can put into orbit a payload whose weight is equal to one or two percent of the thrust of the first-stage rocket booster. The Jupiter-C system which was actually used to put up our first satellite was off optimum and, in addition, used relatively low-performance solid-propellant upper stages. As a result, its ratio of payload weight to booster thrust was an order of magnitude below this optimal value. The Russians were also off optimum in their first satellites, but not quite so far. All of these factors worked in the same direction and thus combined to produce the very large one-hundredfold weight gap between the first few United States satellites and the first few Soviet satellites. By the time we finally got our big boosters working on space applications only a year or so later, this huge temporary gap was reduced to its true value of about twofold.

There was also a time gap, which further confused things. The Russians achieved a long-range flight with an ICBM in August, 1957. We did not achieve the same sort of range until the first full-thrust Atlas launch in December, 1958. Thus, one could say that at that time there was a time gap of sixteen months between the two missile programs. Similarly, if we look at the dates of the first manned orbital flights, April 12, 1961, for Yuri Gagarin and February 20, 1962, for John Glenn, we get a time gap of ten months in these earliest stages of the two man-in-space programs. However, if we look at what happened when we both got beyond the experimental phase and into the operational phase of the program, we find, as is now very well known, a very different story. We deployed a strategically significant missile force well ahead of the Russians, and they did not catch up until almost a decade later. Likewise, we landed a man on the moon in July of 1969, and at this writing we still don't know when they will do the same, or even if they will. Thus, despite appearances and Russian attempts to exploit these appearances, there was no strategically significant missile gap at the time of Sputnik, and when one did develop several years later it was very much in our favor. Sputnik did reveal a space gap, but the real space gap was quite different from the apparent one.

Yet whatever the differences were between the reality and the appearances, the consternation of the American people was real, deep, and widespread. After the first shock, strong reactions set in at all levels and in most segments of American society. After a first futile attempt to belittle the whole affair, the White House caught the general mood and created new organizations and realigned old ones, with the twin purposes of rectifying the past mistake and preventing the occurrence of new ones like it. The Department of Defense did likewise. In the wake of these moves a new wave of scientists and engineers (including me) went to Washington to assume various official positions and replace or reinforce those who had "allowed Sputnik to happen."

The Senate and the House of Representatives created new special committees for similar purposes. The Senate Armed Services Committee, its Preparedness Subcommittee, the Government Operations Committees, the powerful Joint Committee on Atomic Energy, and others all held extensive hearings for the purpose of examining the situation in detail.

Each of the three military services, inspired by a potent mixture of genuine patriotic concern and simple crass opportunism, offered itself up as the means for solving the immediate problem. NACA, the National Advisory Committee for Aeronautics (actually a group of laboratories), did the same, and some in the Atomic Energy Commission suggested that they (like the Joint Committee) stood ready to take the lead in the matter.

The defense industry generally, with an even more potent mix of the same motives, generated a host of new ideas and inventions and dredged up a number of old ones, all for the purpose of reestablishing America's technological leadership in the world and making some money in the process.

The fourth estate quite generally, but especially the kept press of the missile and aviation industries, did its best to keep public concern at a fever pitch and severely castigated whoever it thought was at fault.

PTA's and school boards and university trustees all came to the conclusion that inadequacies in the quality and quantity of science education were the root causes of the whole mess. And as a result the status and salary of nearly all science teachers and professors markedly improved.

Very few, if any, of these science teachers and professors lied about the very tenuous connection between Sputnik and whatever they were doing. But almost all of them were most content with the supposed lessons Sputnik taught, and grim hints could be heard about where the Russians stood in everything from the development of giant accelerators for high-energy nuclear physics to research on the sex habits of the tsetse flies.

After a few weeks of hesitation, the White House reacted positively and sought advice from a broad spectrum of leaders in scientific, technological and other relevant fields about what it all meant and what should be done about it. One of the immediate results of this review was Eisenhower's decision to establish the President's Science Advisory Committee (PSAC), under the chairmanship of James R. Killian, and to establish the position of Special Assistant to the President for Science and Technology, with the same Dr. Killian as its incumbent. (There had been a Science Advisory Committee in the White House Office ever since the Truman administration, but its style of operation and the intensity of its effort were so completely changed that today's committee is best thought of as being established after Sputnik.) Killian had earlier chaired the important Technical Capabilities Panel which made a review of the technological side of our defense posture, and had also been one of the leaders in the Gaither Panel which had conducted a review of our strategic weapons situation just the previous summer. I also participated in a small way in the Gaither Panel and first met Killian during that activity. Killian provided a near-perfect match between the President and other key administrative figures on the one hand and the members of PSAC and other principal scientists and engineering figures on the other hand. He seemed to know precisely what questions to ask the scientists and how to organize their efforts to produce valid answers and usable advice quickly. He was equally skillful in translating this advice into terms that statesmen and high officials could understand and act on.

James B. Fisk of the Bell Telephone Laboratories and Robert F. Bacher of the California Institute of Technology were Vice-Chairmen of the committee. They and practically all of the rest of the members of PSAC had had distinguished careers in pure science. Most had been involved in the administration of important segments of the United States science and technology program (both Fisk and Bacher had held high positions in the AEC in its formative days, and another member, General James H. Doolittle, was at the time the Chairman of NACA). Most of the members had been involved in major projects (radar, atomic weapons, and rockets) during World War II, and most had been members of major advisory committees operating at other high levels of government (for example, I. I. Rabi had been Chairman of the predecessor PSAC, and Kistiakowsky, Wiesner, and I had been members of the Von Neumann Committee). During the first few months after it came into being, from December, 1957, through February, 1958, PSAC was in almost continuous session.

For all practical purposes, the committee was given a free hand to investigate and advise on any scientific and technological matters which the committee itself might decide were important. However, in those first months PSAC also concentrated on the twin goals of determining what to do about the immediate situation and how to prevent its recurrence. It reviewed and analyzed the current technological situations both in the United States and in the Soviet Union, and it advised the President and others as to what in its judgment the Sputniks really meant. Herbert Scoville, then responsible for scientific intelligence at the CIA, regularly sat with the committee in order to assure direct access to all available information concerning Soviet and other foreign technological programs. Working closely with defense officials, but independently of them, the committee reviewed existing programs and urged some changes in them and in their relative priorities. It reviewed some of the flood of new ideas the Soviet successes in space had inspired and urged further study and consideration of some and rejection of others. It studied the whole broad matter of the status, support, and quality of scientific research and of science and engineering education in the United States, and it gave advice which set in motion a number of far-reaching changes in the relationships between government and education of all kinds and at all levels.

Working directly with the new Secretary of Defense, Neil H. McElroy, and with Quarles, then the Deputy Secretary of Defense, Killian and other members of PSAC helped to establish ARPA, the Advanced Research Projects Agency, and helped to arrange my subsequent participation in its direction. ARPA, as we shall see, played an important role in helping the Defense Department keep its house in order in the first months after Sputnik. Working directly with Doolittle and Hugh L. Dryden, PSAC played the major role in designing the plan for transforming NACA (the National Advisory Committee on Aeronautics) into NASA (the National Aeronautics and Space Administration). General Doolittle was the NACA Chairman, and Dryden was its chief operating officer. Dryden became the Deputy Administrator of NASA after it was established by the Congress later in 1958, and Doolittle became one of the members of the National Space Council, another one of the organizational responses to Sputnik.

In retrospect it is clear that PSAC did an extraordinarily important job and exercised good judgment. The organizations which were created largely through its intervention or with its help continue to exist to this day and continue to do the kind of thing that Killian and PSAC outlined for them in those first few months. Most of the programs which PSAC endorsed ultimately did bear fruit and performed useful functions. And we have managed quite well without those programs which PSAC rejected in those early months. It seems very likely that without PSAC the United States in the first frantic responses to the shock of the Russian successes would have undertaken a larger number of ill-advised programs in a more disorganized fashion than we actually did. It is of course not possible to know precisely what the consequences of such additional ill-considered reactions would have been in any detail, but, analogizing from what happened as a result of the excesses that did occur, it seems certain that much money would have been wasted and that genuinely necessary programs would have been slighted and perhaps even left undone.

Meanwhile, in the Department of Defense, similar but more extensive organizational changes were being undertaken for the same purposes. As we have already seen, even before Sputnik, interservice rivalry had led to a quite unnecessary duplication of large, expensive weapons-systems programs. The science and technology apparatus of the Defense Department, especially that part of it in the Office of the Secretary of Defense itself, had proved to be not quite adequate for handling the situation. The frantic reaction Sputnik produced in the military services and among their contractors threatened to cause the situation to get still further out of control. McElroy and Quarles, working with Killian and his committee as well as with their own advisers, generated several new organizational ideas designed to strengthen their ability to manage what threatened to be a very explosive situation. As a first step, they established a new planning and operating agency directly under their control within the immediate Office of the Secretary of Defense. It was called ARPA, the Advanced Research Projects Agency. Roy W. Johnson, a former General Electric executive, was selected to be the first Director of the new agency. Rear Admiral John Clark was named Deputy Director, I was named Chief Scientist, and a few weeks later Lawrence Gise became our Chief Administrative Officer. We began operation in February of 1958 on an unofficial basis, and about one month later we received from the Congress the charter needed to give us a proper legal status. At first ARPA was given two assignments. One was specific: to assume authority over all military space programs. The second was more general and therefore more difficult: to initiate such programs and actions as seemed necessary to avoid another "Sputnik"— i.e., another situation in which the United States suddenly found or even seemed to find itself far behind the principal military competition in some important branch of technology. A third assignment involving taking over the authority and responsibility for the development of the anti–ballistic-missile was also briefly considered. This last was, however, rejected at the behest of the ARPA management itself.

ARPA carried out the first assignment with a reasonable degree of success from the time of its conception in February, 1958, until the fall of 1959. By that latter date, other, better means for controlling the interservice rivalry in this area had come into being and the military space program was parceled out in a rational way among the military services. (Mostly, of course, to the Air Force.)

ARPA carried out the second assignment in part by establishing a number of research and development programs in fields which at the time seemed to be both worthy of support and in danger of falling between the stools insofar as service interest in them was concerned. The most important of these at the time was Project Defender, actually a collection of new ideas, proposals, and research programs related to missile defense.

During the first two years of its life a number of highly placed persons, including General Schriever and former Assistant Secretary of Defense Clifford C. Furnas, called for the abolition of ARPA, but it continues to this day to work on similar programs. The nature of these programs has changed slowly over the years. Some older programs have been transferred to the services as the march of events made that possible, and new ones have been started when that seemed necessary.

In addition to creating ARPA as a kind of ad hoc "quick fix" solution to the problem, the Department of Defense proposed a number of more fundamental organizational changes designed to strengthen its ability to cope with the kind of frantic struggles for new roles and missions that had followed in the wake of Sputnik. The proposals were generated during the early part of 1958 in the executive branch and were enacted by the Congress in the fall of that year as the Defense Reorganization Act of 1958. From the point of view of technology and the arms race, the most important element of that act was the establishment of the position of Director of Defense Research and Engineering. This director was to report directly to the Secretary of Defense and was to function generally at the same level of authority and responsibility as the three service Secretaries. This meant he was to have not only the kind of staff responsibility the other Assistant Secretaries of Defense had, but, in addition, real and direct authority over all research, development, test, and evaluation programs in all components of the Department of Defense, specifically including the three services as well as the new ARPA. I was appointed to the post of Director after two or three other serious candidates turned the job down. (I served under McElroy for the remainder of his term as Secretary of Defense, under

Thomas S. Gates for all of his, and, briefly, in the new Kennedy administration, under Robert McNamara. I resigned then to return to the University of California and was replaced by Harold Brown.) I managed to recruit a number of very fine assistants, including Howard Wilcox, John Rubel, Jack Ruina and Eugene Fubini. Together, with the full support of the Secretary of Defense and with the absolutely essential cooperation of PSAC and its chairmen (at first Killian, then Kistiakowsky, and eventually Wiesner), we gradually got the situation more or less under control. Most of the programs we authorized in that first year or so were ultimately successful, though not always on time and never for the price originally estimated. A few of the programs we authorized were later canceled when it became evident that either they were not really necessary or they were not technically feasible in terms of the then current state of the art. Given the need to be reasonably prudent, and the natural tendency in that position to make some allowance for erring on the side of military safety, I believe our batting average was not too bad. More important, a full decade later, I am not aware of any important program that we disapproved or discontinued where we have any reason to be sorry we did.

The Congress reflected the shock and consternation of the public generally. Its reaction was further complicated by partisan politics.

The Senate, after what appeared to be a few false starts, organized a special committee to look into the matter. It was chaired by Lyndon Johnson, then the Majority Leader. The House similarly established a series of special committees, leading eventually to what is now known as the House Science and Astronautics Committee. Each of these committees held hearings over a period of several years in an effort to come to grips with the problem. They considered the legislative proposals being made by the White House for the establishment of the civil space agency and for the reorganizations in the Department of Defense as discussed just above. Out of this came the legislation which arranged for the transformation of NACA into NASA, as well as the Defense Reorganization Act of 1958 which confirmed the establishment of ARPA and established the office of Director of Defense Research and Engineering.

They considered the programs proposed by these new agencies as well as the programs of the already well-established agencies. They listened to a broad range of witnesses: government officials, high civil servants, contractor personnel, outside advisers and opinion leaders generally. Very early, Lyndon Johnson's committee developed a list of seventeen actions it considered to be essential to maintaining the national security. A number of them related directly to strictly military matters and were designed as a response to the possible "true" missile gap. These included strengthening and dispersing the forces of the Strategic Air Command (SAC), accelerating the installation of a ballistic-missile early-warning system (BMEWS), accelerating all of the missile programs that were close to operational readiness (Atlas, Thor, Jupiter, and Polaris), and intensifying research and development work on the anti–ballistic-missile (ABM). Of special interest nowadays, the Johnson Committee also called for development work on "manned missiles" and on a rocket engine capable of producing one million pounds of thrust. These last two items served no firm military mission at the time, but they did lead directly to the moon landing of 1969.

This seventeen-point list was imperfect, and some of the phraseology supporting it was a bit farfetched, but in retrospect I believe it was superior to any similar list of proposed-action items generated anywhere else in the government at the time. Nearly every one of its proposals was ultimately adopted, and that cannot be said of similar lists prepared by, for instance, the armed services themselves. I find this fact a very reassuring commentary on the relative wisdom of legislators and statesmen vis-à-vis experts (in this case, military men and technologists).

Except for the space-flight items, most of these seventeen actions had been urged by a Senate committee chaired by Stuart Symington the year before, but Sputnik had not yet happened and so they evoked very little response at that time.

The powerful Joint Committee on Atomic Energy saw its primacy as legislative custodian of the most advanced scientific programs in the country threatened by the dawn of the space age. Some of its members first reminded everyone that they had been right in the agreement with J. Robert Oppenheimer over the hydrogen bomb eight years before and also in the argument over the nuclear submarine more recently. They then went on to suggest that the right way to solve the current crisis was through further applications of atomic energy, and they volunteered to assume the legislative responsibility for the entire area. They formed a subcommittee on outer-space propulsion, and they promoted the establishment of a Division of Outer Space Development in the U. S. Atomic Energy Commission. Majority Leader Johnson's actions prevented them from achieving over-all responsibility for space, but they have continued to promote the use of atomic energy as the solution of real and imagined space problems ever since that time. These nuclear solutions include the application of nuclear energy to both rocket propulsion and the production of auxiliary power. It does seem likely that someday nuclear energy will be used for space propulsion, probably in connection with interplanetary flights, and it also seems likely that someday the SNAP (Space Nuclear Auxiliary Power) series of large power plants may become useful in providing power for long-duration flights and for various kinds of equipment that may have a high power demand. But even now, ten years later, most such applications are still premature, and of course in the first year or so after Sputnik they were much more so. They represent classic examples of attempts to find a problem to fit a solution. This approach has in recent years come to characterize a great deal of the work of the Joint Committee on Atomic Energy as well as of the Atomic Energy Commission itself.

Like almost everyone else, the AEC's contractor laboratories receive inspiration from Sputnik. Immediately after that satellite was launched, General Kenneth E. Fields, the General Manager of the AEC, happened to visit the Livermore Laboratory. At that time I was the director of the laboratory, and like so many others I was under the spell of Sputnik and willing to take advantage of its message in a good cause. I played a recording we had made of Sputnik's "beep, beep, beep" as background music during a session in which I pleaded with Fields for some additional budgetary support. I have forgotten what I wanted the additional support for at the time, and I don't know if I ever got it, but I vividly remember the scene itself. Similarly, several years later, Edward Teller, in his perpetual rear-guard battle against nuclear-test bans, solemnly warned, "The probability that a nuclear gap exists right now in addition to a missile gap is frightening and real." In that same time period he was asked what we would find on the moon when we got there and he flatly predicted, "Russians."

Other elements of the bureaucracy even more remote from space and Sputnik discovered how to exploit the missile gap and the resulting public demand that "somebody do something." Thus, we find those responsible for education doing such things as inventing and promoting the National Defense Education Act. Surely we need better education whether we have defense crises or not, but putting in that extra word made the idea sell better; calling it the National Sputnik Education Act would have been, I suppose, too obvious. Similarly, the people with a special interest in and responsibility for highways invented and promoted the National Defense Highway System. I think both of these were intrinsically good ideas, but it is unfortunate that they had to be connected to the missile gap via the word "defense."

The advertising revenue of the aircraft-missile-space press comes almost exclusively from aerospace and related companies searching for new personnel and new contracts, and so it is not surprising that these trade journals did their very best to keep the nation's fears and concerns at a fever pitch. Both in editorials and in supposedly expository articles, they castigated anyone in the executive branch of the government or anywhere else who even hinted at moderation. They predicted the direst future with fleets of Soviet space bombers hanging suspended over the United States and with the Hammer and Sickle plunged into the very cores of the moon and the planets. They conjured up an endless series of other gaps such as the nuclear-airplane gap I discussed earlier. They presented as fact such news items as "Soviet Boost Glide Bomber probably will be towed to 80,000 to 100,000 feet by a ramjet tug." They stated without qualification that the U. S. A. F. Skybolt program was in a race with a similar Soviet program. The missile press also made an outrageous play on words. Science-fiction writers and others had spoken of the conquest of space as one might speak of the conquest of Everest. But the very existence of this phrase was offered as proof of what was going to happen to us all if we didn't wise up. The missile press seemed to have a very simple editorial policy: "If it puts more money into the aerospace business, it's good; if it doesn't, it's bad." Anyone wanting to see examples of dollar patriotism at its worst should read the articles and look at the ads in the various missile journals published during the first two years after Sputnik.

Individual professional men and their societies were not above exploiting the Sputnik fever in their own "good causes." Academic scientists quite frequently in approaching government agencies for funds started out by reminding everyone either of what the Russians were doing or of what we might find them doing if only we knew more about it. I attended a small meeting with President Eisenhower concerning a proposal for a new very large, very expensive nuclear physics accelerator, since built. The briefer, who was not from the laboratory making the proposal, spent most of his time describing the Soviet programs in this very same field. Every word he said was true to the best of his knowledge, and he posed no lurid direct threats to us. Even so, this approach does not seem so different underneath from that of the rocket-industry leader who, in support of expanded spending in his field, said that "tomorrow the country that controls the moon will control the earth."* Similarly, language teachers pointed out *ad nauseam* that much of the important information needed to "catch up" was printed in foreign languages; and on that same basis, computer-software salesmen sold large development programs designed to achieve machine translation of documents.

And the U. S. Soaring Team (gliders) reported after their 1958 International Meet that the U.S.S.R. was making concerted efforts to capture leadership in this field, and they quoted Russian participants as warning, "Wait until 1960."

* A Vice-president of the Glenn L. Martin Company, as quoted in *Aviation Week,* Feb. 10, 1958.

7

MISSILE-GAP MANIA

The reactions of the military services to Sputnik were related to developments which go back to the beginning of the post–World War II period. At that time the Department of the Air Force was set up as a third independent service, and the Department of Defense was established to coordinate and control all three services on behalf of the Commander in Chief, the President of the United States. The Air Force was separated from the Army in part in order to clarify the always difficult question of roles and missions. But in fact the increase in the number of independent claimants for funds only served to confuse things, and the bewilderingly rapid introduction of new weapons resulting from the explosion of technology generated by World War II and its aftermath simply added to the confusion. The Office of the Secretary of Defense, too new, too small, and too weak, could not keep things under control, and the bitter internecine warfare known euphemistically as interservice rivalry soon broke out.

At first this bloodless but bitter and occasionally dirty war involved genuinely substantive issues. These included such questions as the relative value of giant aircraft carriers and long-range bombers in the Atomic Age and such problems as how and by whom air support would be provided to ground troops. However, by 1955 the principal interservice battle had become a power struggle over who would get the juiciest and sexiest roles and missions in long-range missilery and, ultimately, in space.

When Sputnik went up and the "missile gap" came into being, the content of this battle did not much change, but it exploded and completely burst the bonds of good sense and common loyalty that previously had at least partially restrained it. Each of the services, inspired both by genuine patriotic concern and by self-interest, hoped to take advantage of the public confusion and consternation over Sputnik. Supported by its coterie of contractors and special supporting organizations, each intensified its campaign against the other two and against the higher authorities that were trying to restrain the outburst. The battles were fought on the speaking podium, in the kept technological press, and before the committees of Congress.

The Air Force, with much justification, considered the atmosphere and outer space as two parts of the same continuum and proposed that its name be changed to the United States Aerospace Force in recognition of this fundamental unity. Before Sputnik, the Air Force of course had the lion's share of the U. S. long-range missile program and all of the authorized military space programs. But in the summer before Sputnik, an economy wave, generated by Defense Secretary Charles E. Wilson, hit all research and development programs in the Defense Department. Spending on ballistic-missile development was curtailed somewhat, and spending on the Air Force's space programs was affected much more. After Sputnik, the Defense Department, by then under the leadership of McElroy, proposed and the Congress endorsed a supplementary budget which restored reductions in the missile programs and increased the spending rate on the Air Force space programs beyond what it had been earlier. However, the technological content of these programs remained unchanged. The Thor-Agena and Atlas-Agena satellite launchers, both of which were started well before Sputnik, became operational about on their original schedule.

Later on, the program to install a ballistic-missile early-warning system was accelerated to the maximum extent possible, and methods for putting SAC aircraft on the maximum possible level of alert were developed and briefly employed. These actions were taken partly in response to the report of the Johnson Committee and partly in accord with studies made in my office and by the Joint Chiefs of Staff. The rationale behind them was that there might really be a brief period in 1960 or 1961 when the Russians would have a few more ICBMs than we would. As it turned out, such a situation never came about, probably due to the extreme awkwardness of the first Soviet ICBM design, but that could not have been reasonably predicted at the time.

The first successful launch of a military satellite was made on February 28, 1959, when the first of the long series of Discoverer satellites went into orbit. This first Air Force satellite weighed 1,450 pounds and was thus the first United States satellite in a class with Sputnik as far as weight was concerned. These Discoverer satellites were said to be for the purpose of developing various space-flight techniques and checking out engineering designs for such things as maneuver in space and capsule recovery. There were a number of failures at first, but the program was ultimately quite successful and led directly to most of the military satellite programs of today.

A flurry of new proposals for rocket stages using exotic fuels was made, and some old ones were dusted off. After much study and haggling between the Air Force, ARPA, and NASA, these were finally boiled down to one which eventually became the liquid-hydrogen, liquid-oxygen upper stage known as Centaur. After many difficulties and much delay, this unit finally became of use in launching the planetary probes which passed near Venus and Mars.

As another direct consequence of Sputnik and the space fever it induced, the Air Research and Development Command ordered its centers to emphasize exploratory research and development work related to space flight over any such work related to other more earthly Air Force missions. As a result, some hundreds of small study and research programs were started in various more or less exotic fields related to space flight. These included work on ion propulsion and plasma propulsion. These methods of propulsion are, in principle, capable of producing extremely large changes in payload velocity over long times, but they are characterized by having extremely low thrust levels. These characteristics make them useless for launching satellites, but they are potentially valuable for long voyages in interplanetary space. After the first flurry of excitement, it was realized that none of these methods of propulsion was relevant to any of the main-line space programs. Some were dropped, some were continued as long-range exploratory development programs, a few have been tested in space, but none has, even twelve years later, played any significant role in either the military or the civilian space programs. The Air Force also supported studies on controlled thermonuclear propulsion and (with ARPA) on a scheme for using a series of atomic-bomb explosions for lifting huge satellites and space vehicles weighing thousands of tons. The most moderate statement which can be made about these last two bizarre items is that they were grossly premature. The same can be said about similar studies in other exotic fields, including interplanetary communications and moon-based strategic-weapons systems.

But these straightforward development programs in long-range missiles and unmanned satellites plus the basic research, exploratory development, and study programs in advanced and exotic related fields were nowhere near enough to satisfy the appetites stimulated by the missile-gap psychology. The Air Force and its contractors were inspired to invent a number of new weapons systems and dust off some older rejected ideas in efforts to futher expand their activities in missiles and space and to preempt attempts by the other services to do so.

Some of these ideas seemed at the time to have enough

promise to merit going ahead with them at least through an early development phase. One such program was Skybolt. Skybolt was basically an airborne Polaris. Like the Polaris system, it was designed to deliver a thermonuclear warhead to a target some thousand miles from a mobile launching platform. The platform in this case was to be airborne rather than seaborne. Its official *raison d'être* was to extend the "useful life of the bomber force," but it was quite evident that even then Skybolt had an important mission in the interservice battle as well. Early discussions of this new weapon system always compared it to Polaris and attempted to show how it could perform the same missions with greater certainty, in a more timely fashion, and for less money. However, as we proceeded through the early phases of the development program it became evident that the cost estimates and the time estimates for this weapon were much further off than usual, and it was ultimately canceled.

Dyna-Soar was the second major weapon system that was given a chance to proceed through the first steps of development. It was an archetype of the old rejected idea permitted a new lease on life in the frantic early post-Sputnik era. In concept, Dyna-Soar was a kind of hypersonic manned aircraft designed to be boosted up to very nearly orbital speed by a large rocket. After reaching such speeds, it was to skip along the top of the atmosphere, pass over its target, and then fly back down to its home base. Unlike a simple missile nose cone, it was to be able to use its rudimentary wings and other airfoils to achieve a limited amount of maneuverability.

A project rather similar to Dyna-Soar had been proposed to the German government during World War II. During the Sputnik fever, General Dornberger, one of the Operation Paper Clip group and then employed by Bell Aviation, worked very hard to sell this idea in the United States. He once testified that he had made some nine hundred (that is the number I recall) presentations to all sorts of committees and other bodies in an effort to get Dyna-Soar approved, but that he had been unable to get what he called a "decision." His story was designed to show that the United States government was terribly indecisive, but all it proved to me was how remarkably persistent Dornberger was.

It very soon became obvious that Dyna-Soar—like Skybolt, only more so—would cost far more than the early estimates, that it would take much longer to accomplish, and that its ostensible purposes could all be achieved more readily and more cheaply by other means. The program was therefore severely cut back in 1960 and finally canceled completely in 1963.

In retrospect, I think we were right to give the Skybolt designers a chance to proceed through the early phases of development. It might have worked out and it might have served a useful purpose. Indeed, I regard it as possible that we will someday go back to something like it when and if the technological situation changes enough to justify it. I feel very differently about Dyna-Soar. In retrospect, I think we should have recognized at the beginning that it was a nonsensical program. I played an important part in allowing it to get started and I regard it as one of my major errors.

Other post-Sputnik program ideas which the Air Force tried to sell to higher authorities were recognized as unfeasible or unnecessary early enough so they never got beyond the study stage. Such ideas include the "Aerospace Plane." Instead of being launched into space by a large booster which would then be discarded, the Aerospace Plane was to fly directly into orbit from a normal ground takeoff. In flight, as its speed increased, it was to change from a form of propulsion suitable at lower velocities to others suitable at higher velocities, and so on until high altitudes and orbital velocity were reached. The idea was far beyond the state of the art in many of the relevant technological fields, and thus grossly premature to say the least.

The Air Force also strongly promoted the idea that we should undertake on an urgent basis the development and deployment of a "satellite interceptor," to be known as SAINT. The President himself, in recognition of the fact that we didn't want anybody else interfering with our satellites, limited this program to "study only" status and ordered that no publicity be given either the idea or the study of it. The other two military departments independently promoted the same idea and volunteered their services for its accomplishment.

Another far-out idea was Bambi, a space-based anti–ballistic-missile system. The concept of this mad-scientist's-dream involved surrounding the earth with a great swarm of small satellites that would detect, attack, and destroy anything that stuck its nose above the atmosphere. Some thought had been given to the question of how to enable friendly missiles and satellites to pass through the swarm, but that was one of the least of the problems with this system, and it too never got beyond the study stage.

The Air Force also managed, with some success, to apply the post-Sputnik gap psychology to other systems, such as the B-70 and the nuclear airplane (ANP) as described earlier. The budgets supporting the development of these weapons systems were temporarily expanded in the reaction to Sputnik, even though they were only peripherally connected with space. Like almost everything else that moved, they were, for a time, proposed as launching platforms for satellites.

Other similar ideas were put forward. A number of these, like Dyna-Soar and the Aerospace Plane, involved getting Air Force pilots into space. This basic goal was pursued with great zeal and emotion. Both specific and general rationalizations supporting the need for military man in space were advanced. All of the rationalizations that were based on having the man perform some specific military function were found to be faulty. Either the function could be better performed within the atmosphere than above it or it could be better performed by an unmanned satellite than by a manned one. The generalized rationalization that man was more "flexible" was, of course, true, but its relevance to the Air Force's space missions was never clearly established. Furthermore, saying that a man's judgment is necessary somewhere in a military space system is *not* tantamount to saying he is needed in the part of the system that actually orbits. In a great many cases, even though not all, he can perform his function just as well or better in the ground control room than in the orbiting capsule. This argument was settled the year after Sputnik by giving the general-purpose man-in-space mission to the civilian space agency, NASA. However, Air Force boosters were of necessity used to launch NASA's manned satellites. The Mercury capsules were launched into orbit by a slightly modified Atlas, and the Gemini capsules were launched by a modified Titan II, which was in turn a considerably uprated and modified version of the Titan I. Only the later Apollo spacecraft were orbited by rockets not originally designed to function as long-range missiles. Air Force officers have played a very important role in the management of all these programs, and, of course, Air Force test pilots, along with Navy and Marine pilots and a few civilians, have manned many spacecraft. But the Air Force has never given up on having a space-flight program all its own, as demonstrated by the on-again, off-again MOL (Manned Orbiting Laboratory) program later on in the sixties.

What became of all the new ideas born out of the reactions to Sputnik? Where did they lead us? What did they contribute to our security in general and to closing the missile gap in particular? The surprising, perhaps unbelievable, yet most significant answers to these three questions are: Nothing, nowhere, nothing. All of the long-range missiles deployed in the dozen years following Sputnik were the product either of programs originated before Sputnik or of programs derived directly from such earlier ones. Similarly, with only minor exceptions, all military space programs and satellite launchers are derived directly from programs initiated and worked out in considerable detail before Sputnik. Virtually all the new programs that came into being in the burst of inventive activity inspired by Sputnik and the "missile gap" all came to a dead end sooner or later. Nor did they produce any really important "technological fallout" (a term invented to justify expenditures on programs which cannot be justified as ends in themselves). To put it simply, large amounts of money and human effort were wasted in a wild pursuit of the exotic.

The Navy too made a grab for a bigger piece of the action in long-range missiles and space. It did already have a small foothold consisting of the Polaris program and some major range facilities in southern California. However, the poor showing it made in the Vanguard program hamstrung efforts to expand this foothold, even though much of the blame for this fiasco belonged elsewhere. When the first Russian satellite went into orbit sooner than even most space buffs expected, the Vanguard Program Office was pressured to accelerate its schedule and to try to advance its launch date by several months. As a result, it failed in its first tries to achieve orbit in the months immediately following Sputnik. Eventually it did put into orbit some very tiny instrument packages, one of which is still there. As a counter to the Air Force proposal that it become the Aerospace Force, the Navy pointed out that since the earliest days of science fiction people had spoken of space*ships*. And we all know who is responsible for ships, don't we? (It is possible that the Navy, unlike the Air Force, offered this argument with tongue in cheek.) The Navy also argued that there were a number of advantages in launching satellites from the sea that were not available otherwise. These included a much greater flexibility in choosing the latitude of the launch and the launch azimuth, and also a much greater possibility for secretly launching satellites should this be desired. In my opinion all of these claims were true but none of them were of sufficient relevance or value to justify spending large sums on the development of a sea launch capability.

The Navy did have one satellite proposal which was both important and of special Navy interest. This was for a navigational-aid satellite known as Transit. It proceeded with that program, using Air Force launches, and turned in an excellent and useful job. With that one exception, the missile and space ideas and projects generated by the Navy and its laboratories and contractors in their first quick response to Sputnik all came to naught, just as in the case of the Air Force. However, the amount of money and effort wasted was one tenth as large.

In accordance with the report of Senator Johnson's committee and also with studies sponsored by the Joint Chiefs of Staff and my office, the Navy did accelerate its Polaris program and succeeded in moving the operational-readiness date forward by several months.

In the case of the Army, the situation was extremely complicated and it took a long time and a great expenditure of nervous energy to work out a solution that finally made sense.

At the time Sputnik was launched, the Army was still working on the development of the Jupiter IRBM, but operational control of this missile had already been assigned to the Air Force by Secretary Wilson in 1956. The future of this program, at one time the Army's white hope in the space race, looked bleak indeed. The Army also was working on the Nike-Zeus anti–ballistic-missile system. This was a complex system and it challenged the abilities of many good engineers, but Nike-Zeus was an *antimissile* missile and it had only a relatively short range despite its very large thrust. No matter how it might make out as an end in itself, it did not look promising as a steppingstone to space, and that was what the Medaris–Von Braun team was really interested in.

This gloomy picture changed radically in the first few months after Sputnik. Following Sputnik, and after Vanguard's

initial failure, the authorization to use the bootlegged Jupiter
C to attempt to launch America's first satellite was eagerly
given. Jupiter C, with its name changed to Juno I when it was
used for this purpose, did so on the very first try in January,
1958. (By chance it happened that in early December, 1957,
I was Chairman of the subpanel of the President's Science Advisory Committee charged with assessing the probability of
success of the Vanguard and the Juno I. After an intensive
week's study, we informed the President that the Juno I had
a fifty-fifty chance of success on the first try and that the Vanguard had only a fifty-fifty chance of ever getting anything up.
This prediction turned out to be very close to the mark: the
first Juno I launch attempt was successful and the second
failed; Vanguard finally achieved orbit only after a long delay
and much anguish.)

Whether the achievement of launching thirty-one pounds in
January, 1958, with Juno I justified the almost subversive actions necessary to do so is something which, in retrospect, I
am not at all sure about. This kind of clever maneuvering in
which ambitious men work out ways of getting around the
restraints imposed by a higher authority, including authority
at the constitutional level, goes on all the time in all the
services and without doubt constitutes one of the most powerful driving forces behind the arms race. In this case, as in
some others, it was hailed and rewarded after the fact. But
even at the time it was clear that the Air Force satellite program could, within a year or so, put well over a thousand
pounds into orbit, and in fact on February 28, 1959, the Air
Force's Thor-Agena launched Discoverer I, weighing 1,450
pounds. Also, the ARPA–Air Force Project Score resulted in
placing an entire Atlas in orbit in December of 1958. The
true useful payload was relatively small, and the project can
be properly classified as a stunt, but the total weight in orbit
included the entire ten-thousand-pound Atlas carcass. To the
extent that getting something big into orbit was the name of

the game, Score was a resounding success. But, more importantly, from a technological point of view, it is almost certain that today's satellites and space vehicles would not be very different from what they in fact are if there had never been a Jupiter C/Juno I. However, it was perhaps inevitable that these successes would be rewarded no matter what their origins, and eventually they were to a degree.

Meanwhile, the massive reorganizations described earlier were moving ahead. NACA was being converted into NASA, and in the process it acquired the responsibility for all civilian space programs, including manned space flight and exploration. ARPA was established in the Office of the Secretary of Defense and given the responsibility for all the military space programs.

In the early months before NASA really got moving, ARPA determined that among other things the military space program was going to need a first-stage booster several times the size of Atlas or Titan and a second-stage booster to be fueled with liquid hydrogen. ARPA assigned the development of the big first-stage booster to the Medaris–Von Braun group, and the development of the liquid-hydrogen stage was assigned to the Air Force, which, in turn, eventually contracted it out to General Dynamics/Astronautics. As a result of some subsequent horse trading, the hydrogen second stage (which eventually became known as the Centaur) became for a time the administrative responsibility of NASA, and the large first-stage booster (which eventually became the Saturn I) remained the administrative responsibility of ARPA. Considering that by then NASA already had been assigned the general-purpose man-in-space mission, I felt that the arrangement was backwards, but from my position as Chief Scientist of ARPA I was unable to do anything about it.

This set of circumstances, reorganizations, and program decisions created a most anomalous situation. First, Von Braun, who worked for the Army, was in charge of the development of the biggest United States booster, the Saturn, but the Army had no approved role in space. (Army missile spokesmen urgently pointed out a number of times that the moon was high *ground,* but no one took the hint.) Second, ARPA had administrative authority over the Saturn, but, with no approved military manned space program in sight, it had no known application for that booster. Third, NASA had the legal responsibility for the only authorized man-in-space program, but it had no authority over the development of the very big boosters ultimately necessary for it.

This anomaly created much confusion within the government and the country at large. The press and the Congress, with much justification, castigated the Administration for creating and permitting such a confused situation. As time went on, tempers frayed further and the power struggle became more severe. The confusion inherent in this arrangement began to create a real drag on the program as a whole and prevented a number of needed decisions from being made. The whole matter soon came to be widely characterized as a "mess."

Quarles and T. Keith Glennan, the first Administrator of NASA, worked out the most sensible of all the suggestions of how to straighten out the mess. In the fall of 1958 they proposed that the space-oriented part of the Army Ballistic Missile Agency (that is, for all practical purposes, the Von Braun group) and the Jet Propulsion Laboratory (JPL) of the California Institute of Technology be transferred from the Department of the Army to the fledgling NASA. The JPL, under the direction of William Pickering, had been an integral part of the Juno-I team. While the Von Braun organization had been responsible for the first-stage booster and for systems integration and launch, JPL had been responsible for the design and development of the upper stages of that first U. S. satellite launcher as well as for the satellite itself. This transfer proposal made eminently good sense: the President and the

Congress had assigned the mission for space exploration in the broadest sense to Glennan's organization, and these two groups were the most qualified of any immediately available for participating in the mission. Other groups, which had more or less the same qualifications, such as the Space Technology Laboratory, were right then deeply involved in some of the "highest-priority" military programs discussed earlier. The Department of the Army, meaning especially General Medaris and Secretary Brucker, did not take kindly to this proposal, and they fought it tooth and nail. By claiming that the Von Braun team was also involved in other essential Army missile programs in a way that made it impossible to split them off from the rest of the Army Ordnance and Missile Command, the Secretary of the Army was able to block that part of the transfer proposal. JPL was transferred to NASA in due time, but the transfer of JPL alone, while useful and sensible, was entirely inadequate as a solution to the basic problem, and so public and Congressional criticism continued to mount.

Each of the three military departments proposed its own solution to the problem. The Air Force suggested that the responsibility for all military space programs be turned over to it but not necessarily with the people then in charge of them. The Navy proposed that a military space command, in which it would have a full one-third share, be established. The Army (again meaning really General Medaris and Secretary Brucker) suggested that a joint space and missile command be established and gallantly offered to turn Medaris, Von Braun and much of the rest of the Huntsville group and facilities over to it to set it up and run it. None of these proposals was acceptable to anyone beyond those making them, and so things continued for a time to remain as they were.

In the meantime, I had become Director of Defense Research and Engineering and thus acquired authority over all elements of the space program within the Department of Defense. I reviewed the whole space program, including especially the anomalous situation described above, and made two recommendations. The first was to Defense Secretary McElroy and was to the effect that the responsibility for developing all military-satellite launchers and for making all military-satellite launches should be transferred to the Air Force; that except for certain specifically named exceptions all military-satellite-payload development be made the responsibility of the Air Force; and that the responsibilities and authorities of ARPA in military space programs be discontinued. McElroy accepted the recommendation, and a directive to this effect was issued late in the summer of 1959. My second recommendation was more far-reaching and had to go to the President and T. Keith Glennan, the Administrator of NASA, as well as to the Secretary of Defense for final implementation. In brief, at a meeting in the White House in late October, 1959, attended by the President, McElroy, Gates, Glennan, Dryden, General Nathan F. Twining, Chairman of the Joint Chiefs of Staff, and Kistiakowsky, I recommended that (1) administrative responsibility for the Saturn booster be transferred from the Department of Defense (ARPA) to NASA, where the responsibility for manned space flight already was, and (2) that the Von Braun group be transferred to NASA along with the Saturn program. McElroy, Glennan, and the President accepted this recommendation, and transfers of authority and personnel were made a few months later.

One might have thought that that would have settled the matter, but it didn't. The Army, as was right and proper, continued to be responsible for the Nike-Zeus anti–ballistic-missile (ABM) system. It had been arranged to have Zeus test equipment installed at Kwajalein Atoll in the mid-Pacific. It had been further arranged that the Air Force would launch targets for testing this equipment from Vandenberg Air Force Base in California, using ICBM boosters to do so. Suddenly, I learned that General Medaris had proposed that the Zeus equipment at Kwajalein be tested by firing test targets from

Johnson Island in the mid-Pacific. Since this was closer to Kwajalein than California was, the launch could be made with the Jupiter IRBM booster. This proposal was supported by all sorts of technical claims about why this was a better and more appropriate way to do things. Jack Ruina, the Assistant Director of Defense Research and Engineering for Air Defense, and I examined the question closely and determined that none of these claims made good sense upon careful examination. I could only assume that the whole thing was simply another last-minute attempt to save Jupiter. In keeping with my authority over all defense research and development programs, I disapproved this part of the Zeus test program.

The last Jupiters planned for deployment in Turkey and Italy were just about to come off the line at the Chrysler plant, and the people there, of course, had a very great interest in keeping it going. Shutting down the Jupiter production lines at Chrysler would result in terminating the employment of thousands of persons in the months immediately preceding the Presidential election of 1960, and Michigan was a key state. The White House therefore told Secretary Gates and me to check with Vice-President Nixon, the presumed candidate of the Republican Party in the forthcoming election, before doing anything so drastic. We did so, and I'm pleased to be able to say that Mr. Nixon, without a moment's hesitation, told us to do whatever was right in our judgment without reference to politics.

At one point in this long controversy, Army Secretary Brucker called me to his office and arranged a scene I shall never forget. He sat behind his desk, facing the center of the room. He put me in a large stuffed chair to the left of his desk, and a colonel with a pad and a pen ostentatiously poised over it took up a position behind me. The Chief of Staff of the United States Army, the Deputy Chief of Staff, and the Chief of Research and Development, eleven stars in all, were arrayed in seats along the front of the Secretary's desk, facing him. Richard S. Morse, the civilian Director of Research and Development for the Army, sat next to the generals. General Medaris paced the floor on the other side of the room. Secretary Brucker did most of the talking. He told me what he thought of my decisions and he repeatedly threatened me by saying, "Wait till the people hear what you're trying to do, wait till the Congress hears what you're trying to do."

Once or twice I made a remark designed to explain some part of my position, but the only response I evoked was from Medaris, and he didn't say anything. He just shook his head in wonder, walked over to the window, and looked up into the heavens pleadingly. I did feel a bit overwhelmed at first, but a measure of personal vanity which I suppose I share with nearly everyone sustained me. All the while the Secretary threatened me and scolded me, a thought kept circulating in my head: "He's the Secretary of the Army, he's furious about what I'm doing, but I'm on leave from the University of California and there's nothing this poor so-and-so can do to me that I care about, and he knows it." The only external evidence of his threat was a small item which appeared in *Newsweek* during this tense period. It said I was a registered Democrat, an egghead, and one of those scientists who were trying to run things. I remarked later to Lloyd Norman, who had written the item, that the first charge was true, I supposed the second was, and the Defense Reorganization Act of 1958 said I was supposed to behave in accord with the third.

This impasse between Brucker and me created a dilemma for Secretary of Defense Thomas S. Gates. He therefore asked George Kistiakowsky, then the President's science adviser and Chairman of PSAC, to look into the matter and tell him what was right. Kistiakowsky established a panel to do so. After hearing arguments from all of us, the panel and Kistiakowsky supported my view, and the Jupiter program, which should never have been started in the first place, was at long last laid to rest.

General Medaris resigned from the Army and became the president of the Lionel Corporation (which makes toy electric trains). There his immediate boss was Board Chairman Roy M. Cohn, the same Cohn who had been one of the first Senator McCarthy's two chief aides and as such had given a very bad time to other Army generals and to the then Secretary of the Army. The General Counsel of the Department of Defense at the time of those McCarthy hearings was none other than Wilber Brucker. One of the reasons he was later appointed Secretary of the Army was that he had performed well in connection with the hearings. I've always thought of the whole interconnected complex set of events as a kind of cosmic political joke of the same genre as Khrushchev's naming Molotov ambassador to Outer Mongolia after he had served as Foreign Minister of the U.S.S.R. for many years.

Soon after his resignation Medaris wrote a book called *Countdown for Decision*. In it he gives his version of the story I have recounted above. He charges that there were at the time a number of serious deficiencies in the decision-making structure of the Department of Defense. It will surprise no one by now to learn that he thought I ranked high among them.

As in the case of the Air Force, all these efforts of the Army missile people to carve out a space mission for themselves not only wasted large sums of the public's money, but also diverted money and attention from other Army programs where there was a serious need for them. In this context, General Nathan Twining, then Chairman of the Joint Chiefs of Staff, was quoted as asking, "Are these research and development programs, which are certainly limited dollarwise, directed properly to providing a compact, hard-hitting Army?" There were rumblings to this same effect within the Army itself, but the extraordinarily close relationship of Brucker, Medaris, and Von Braun prevented them from rising to the surface.

In addition to the three services, other elements of the Department of Defense acted under the heady influence of the missile-gap psychology. ARPA contained almost as many Bambi enthusiasts as did the Air Force, and one of Roy Johnson's last acts as Director of ARPA was an attempt to persuade the Congress that the United States needed to get to work on an orbital bombardment system. Fortunately, neither the Congress nor the Air Force picked up this basically poor idea, and the U. S. public has been spared paying for it.

A slightly more sensible idea, a *fractional* orbital bombardment system, or FOBS, was developed by the Soviets in the late sixties. In FOBS, a warhead is launched into a low orbit which would take it clear around the earth if undisturbed, but before it can make one full turn the warhead is given a new impulse which causes it to reenter the atmosphere. Both the accuracy and the payload are degraded by this series of additional maneuvers. In just plain OBS, the situation is worse. In the course of making many repeated orbits, a satellite passes over all points on the ground lying between its northernmost and southernmost latitudes. Unless it is in an equatorial orbit (and that shouldn't bother *us*), only once or twice a day does its orbit take it over or near any particular area which might contain its target. On other turns, it *cannot* pass over these same points. To take an extreme case, at the time it is at the longitude of New York, it may be at the latitude of Santiago, Chile. Thus it cannot in general be given a sufficient impulse to direct it to its target except during certain short predetermined intervals. Hence it is a very poor weapon for any military situation where massive surprise or quick response might be needed. It suffers from other defects, too, and in general is quite inferior to the much simpler ICBM as a weapon. Still, the idea of bombs orbiting directly overhead, as if they were somehow analogous to Damocles' sword, can be quite scary to people having no understanding of Newton's laws or of how orbits work, and so it does keep coming up.

In summary of the last two chapters, what effect did Sputnik have on the United States?

1. Several long-lasting organizational inventions were introduced. Most important among these were the creation of PSAC and a Special Assistant to the President for Science and Technology at the White House level, the creation of the civilian space agency NASA at a level equivalent to that of the Cabinet departments, the creation of ARPA and the office of the DDRE in the Department of Defense, and the creation of certain committees and subcommittees of the Congress designed to deal more adequately with scientific and technological problems. In my judgment, all of these new organizations have been very useful and all have by and large done a good job.

2. The status and the salaries of most scientists and many types of engineers substantially increased. Many sub-Cabinet jobs are now filled by scientists and engineers; such was not the case before Sputnik. Science education from kindergarten through the university received special attention from PTA's, school boards, and university trustees. Support of graduate education was greatly stimulated in all fields, but especially in science, through federal contracts and grants.

3. The missile gap, which was what all the fuss was supposed to be about, was, for all practical purposes, unaffected, except that some funds which had been cut in an economy wave just before Sputnik were restored. By the time a strategically significant number of missiles had been deployed, the missile gap was in our favor, and it took the Russians almost a decade to catch up. But the development programs that led to that state of affairs were initiated well before Sputnik. Even the weapons that our current (1970) strategic posture is based on are the result of development programs either started before Sputnik or directly derived from programs that were. Surprising as it may seem, the wild outbursts of ideas inspired by Sputnik and the missile-gap psychology has produced nothing of direct value to our current strategic posture more than twelve years later.

4. Our military space programs were accelerated somewhat, but otherwise were only slightly affected by Sputnik and the missile-gap psychology. As in the case of our current strategic-weapons forces, our current military space programs are virtually all based on ideas which were current before Sputnik. And the development programs designed to exploit these ideas either were started before Sputnik or grew directly out of programs that were. A few of the booster stages now used in our military space programs are the result of developments initiated after Sputnik, but of course it is not possible to say whether even these are truly a direct consequence of it.

5. The effect of Sputnik on our civilian space program is a quite different matter. The creation of the civilian space agency NASA was itself a direct reaction to Sputnik, and the bulk of the civil space program, including manned space flight and lunar and planetary exploration, is a direct consequence of Sputnik and our first reactions to it. Had there been no Sputnik, manned space flight almost certainly would have developed in a natural way as a part of our military space program. However, since the first military space satellites were all designed to be automatic rather than manned, it's not possible to predict when this would have happened. Even so, I am willing to conjecture that the first orbital flight would have happened in the early sixties, within a year or so of when it actually did. On the other hand, it is very doubtful that we would have reached the moon during the sixties without the intense stimulation of Sputnik and the shock it produced.

6. The sudden establishment of new development programs and research projects in the aftermath of Sputnik further stretched our resources beyond the already taut situation created by the excessive pre-Sputnik programs. Many good people were diverted from necessary but more mundane tasks to new, exotic ones. There was excessive job switching at all levels, inspired by ads emphasizing rapid advancement, independence, and technical challenge, and many in the higher

echelons walked off the job in search of a new El Dorado called Capital Gains. The relatively low level of reliability of some of our early missiles and space launchers was, without doubt, in part due to all of this turmoil, as was the excessive number of design bugs discovered later in the programs than they should have been. It was my pleasure to know personally many of the top leaders in our most important weapons and space programs, and I can assert that they put out truly heroic efforts, but there can't be any doubt they were stretched too thin for optimum performance.

7. Programmatic reactions to Sputnik served to accelerate the arms race even though the burst of ideas produced by the missile-gap psychology did not in the end produce any useful military hardware. They did produce a still bigger defense industry and hence a still bigger political constituency in support of weapons development. This, in turn, strengthened those elements of the Congress that automatically endorsed any weapons-development program, and tipped the Congressional balance of power still further in that direction. Very soon after Sputnik we reached a point where the Armed Services Committees of the Congress commonly castigated the Department of Defense for the weapons programs it didn't support, but seldom examined critically those it did support. This situation continued throughout the sixties until failures in Vietnam reduced public confidence in the absolute wisdom of the military mind and permitted critical Congressional review of the anti–ballistic-missile and other programs.

8

THE McNAMARA ERA

After the election of John F. Kennedy, the term "missile gap" soon disappeared. The continuing flow of new intelligence information confirmed that the Soviets were not translating their lead in ICBM development into a corresponding lead in missile deployment. More important, the term had been pretty much taken over by the Democrats as a campaign criticism of the Eisenhower Administration, and the political utility of such charges disappeared with the election of the new Administration. Despite common expectations and some misguided but fervent hopes to the contrary, the changeover in administration was marked by continuity and consolidation insofar as the strategic-arms race was concerned. This continuity, in turn, was due in part to the fact that any sensible technological approach to the strategic-arms problem was bound to produce more or less the same solution. Even more importantly, many of the persons who had played the principal roles in formulating these policies under Eisenhower continued to do so in the new Kennedy Administration.

The new Secretary of Defense, Robert S. McNamara, invited all five of the research and development officials at the Presidential-appointee level to stay on, and four of us did. Besides myself, this group included Dr. Joseph V. Charyk, the Undersecretary of the Air Force; Dr. James H. Wakelin, Jr., the Assistant Secretary of the Navy for Research and Development; and Richard S. Morse, the Director of Research and Development for the Army. I had agreed to stay on only for a few months in order to help make the transition in government as smooth as possible and to give the new Secretary plenty of time to find the kind of man he considered suitable as my replacement. And on May first I was replaced by my good friend and long-time colleague Harold Brown. The other holdovers had no plans for leaving soon, and in fact most of them stayed on for protracted periods.

In addition, all of my senior staff stayed on and two of them were promoted by Robert McNamara to positions of greater responsibility and authority. My principal deputy, John Rubel, was given the additional title of Assistant Secretary of Defense (Deputy Director of Research and Engineering). That title had been unused since the enactment of the Defense Reorganization Act of 1958. Jack P. Ruina, who had been my Assistant Director for Air Defense, became the Director of the Advanced Research Projects Agency, ARPA, succeeding Brigadier General Austin R. Betts, who had left a few weeks earlier to become the Director of the Division of Military Applications in the Atomic Energy Commission.

This continuity of top personnel in science and engineering was in marked contrast to what happened in other areas. With only one exception, the twenty-odd nonscientific members of the Defense secretariat were all replaced at the very beginning of the new administration.

Much the same thing happened in 1961 in the case of the White House science apparatus. Jerome Wiesner became President Kennedy's Special Assistant for Science and Technology. He had been one of the members of Killian's original PSAC and he was a close associate of both Killian and George Kistiakowsky, his immediate predecessors. His views were basically very similar to theirs. The President's Science Advisory Committee itself, as usual, held over all but a very few of its seventeen members. The committee, in accordance with custom, also elected Wiesner its Chairman. A new unit named the Office of Science and Technology was soon established in the Executive Office of the President, but this did not indicate a change. Wiesner was its Director. Some of the men who had been the principal members of the Special Assistant's staff during the Eisenhower administration became part of the staff of this new unit in the Kennedy administration. Among the holdovers were David Z. Beckler and Spurgeon Keeny. Beckler has served from the beginning as de-facto chief executive officer of the White House science apparatus. Keeny later also served simultaneously as an assistant to both McGeorge Bundy and Walt W. Rostow when they in turn were Special Assistants to the President for National Security Affairs. (To jump way ahead of our story, we may note that in 1969 when Nixon succeeded Johnson there was a broader and deeper change in the White House science apparatus: Nixon's new science adviser, Lee DuBridge, had not been a major participant in political affairs for many years prior to his appointment, and Spurgeon Keeny, who had been an important factor in maintaining continuity earlier during the 1961 change of administration, moved over in 1969 to the Arms Control and Disarmament Agency as its Assistant Director for Science and Technology.)

Because of the continuity of people in 1961, it was to be expected that there would be no revolutionary changes in our strategic-weapons development and deployment programs. And there were none. The Atlas development and deployment program was continued very nearly as it had been originally planned, and eventually about one hundred missiles were deployed. The first few Atlas squadrons were stored above ground in a horizontal position in concrete coffins that provided some protection against blast damage. In order to launch the early missiles it was necessary first to hoist them into a vertical position and, after they were erect, to fill their tanks with several tens of thousands of gallons of fuel and liquid oxygen.

Later versions of Atlas, like all present-day ICBMs, were stowed in concrete-lined underground silos designed to protect them against nearby nuclear explosions. These silos were able to withstand some hundreds of pounds per square inch of overpressure. (A one-megaton bomb exploded on the ground produces a blast overpressure of one hundred pounds per square inch at a distance of about six tenths of a mile from ground zero.) These silo-based Atlases also had to be fueled at the last minute, just like the earlier ones. The fueling process plus other last-minute adjustments were supposed to be accomplished in only fifteen minutes. This time was just short of the maximum warning time that could then be expected in the event of a surprise missile attack. It was, of course, much shorter than the warning time available in the case of a bomber attack. However, subsequent tests and exercises gave results which, in my mind, make it very doubtful that we could have gotten even one in five of the early operational Atlases off in that time under surprise-attack conditions.

During the early sixties, the Atlas went through a number of modifications designed to improve readiness and delivery accuracy, but the system was awkward in a fundamental way and the last Atlas missiles were decommissioned in the mid-sixties.

At the time of President Kennedy's inauguration there were two distinct Titan development programs under way. The older version, the Titan I, had basically the same performance characteristics as Atlas and used the same fuels. It differed principally in that it employed the more nearly ideal two-stage design. This made it somewhat less awkward than the Atlas, but it still shared the same fundamental deficiency of requiring that its liquid oxygen, or LOX as it is usually called, be supplied just before launch.

The other version of this missile is known as the Titan II.

Its development was started about four years later than the Titan I, and it was consequently based on a later and more advanced state of the art. It weighs about fifty percent more than the Titan I, the thrust of its engines is also about fifty percent greater, and its payload-carrying capability is correspondingly larger. But more important for military applications, it uses an entirely different fuel-and-oxidizer combination. The fuel, UDMH, is a derivative of a toxic nitrogen compound, hydrazine. The oxidizer is nitrogen textroxide. Both are poisonous and nasty to handle, but they have the twin advantages of being liquids under normal temperature conditions and of igniting directly on contact. Such fuel–oxidizer combinations which ignite on contact are spoken of as being "hypergolic," and combinations which can be stored without the use of extreme refrigeration or high pressures are known as "storable." The use of this storable hypergolic propellant combination enables the Titan II to be stored in its silo fully fueled and ready to go. It also makes possible a somewhat simpler and hence more reliable engine design. The Titan II development program had always been surrounded by controversy. I had favored it, and so had General Schriever, but not all of our technical and military colleagues had. However, after a review of the Titan program, the new Administration decided to continue its development as previously laid out, but to reduce the number of planned Titan II squadrons by one. Eventually all of the Titan Is were decommissioned, but in 1970 there were still fifty-four Titan IIs deployed as part of our strategic forces.

The Atlas and the Titan II performed major service as boosters in our civilian and military satellite programs throughout the 1960s. The Atlas was used to launch the one-man Mercury capsules which initiated our manned-space-flight program. The Titan II was used to launch the two-man Gemini capsules which made possible the docking experiments and the space-walk experiments which led directly to our Apollo program. With some additional solid-propellant boosters strapped on in parallel with its first stage to give it still greater initial thrust, the Titan II became the Titan III and was used to launch satellites into extremely high orbits.

The Minuteman ICBM was, of course, also inherited from the Eisenhower Administration, having been started in 1957 just before Sputnik. The Minuteman was, as already described, a three-stage solid-propellant rocket. Its payload was considerably less than that of either the Atlas or the Titan, but it could be stored indefinitely in a ready-to-go status and launched on approximately a one-minute warning to targets which had been previously stored in the memory bank of its inertial-guidance system.

Like the Atlas and the Titan, the Minuteman was to be deployed in underground silos, but, since the whole system was smaller and less complex, it was easy to make the silos stronger than in the case of the big liquid missiles. These days the figure "300 pounds p.s.i. hardness" is commonly used to describe the degree of protection which the underground silos give to the Minuteman. This number means that in order to destroy a Minuteman rocket in its silo an attacking weapon must land close enough to produce a blast overpressure of three hundred pounds per square inch. For example, a one-megaton ground burst must be within about two thousand feet of the entrance to the silo in order to destroy its contents. At the time of the changeover in administration, Secretary Gates had not yet determined the ultimate number of Minutemen to be deployed, but he had set in motion programs designed to provide facilities for manufacturing and reworking a force of somewhat less than 1,000, the precise number depending on the rates involved. The Air Force, on the other hand, was urging deployment figures more like 2,000 to 3,000, and General Thomas S. Power, then commander of SAC, talked of 10,000.

McNamara resolved these uncertainties early in his administration. He set the deployment goal at first at 800 and then soon after increased it to 1,000. He also increased somewhat the size of the manufacturing and reworking facilities. There had also been a plan to build a rail-mobile version of Minuteman, but McNamara canceled that too within the first six months of his administration.

Minuteman has steadily evolved as new components and new operational concepts have been developed since 1960. The Minuteman III now (1970) being deployed will hurl a larger payload a longer distance and will do so with much finer accuracy than the original version of this weapon. The warhead of the Minuteman III is scheduled to be a MIRV (multiple independently targetable reentry vehicles). During the public ABM debate of 1969, the Minuteman MIRV was said to consist of three independently guided warheads of two hundred kilotons explosive power each.

The Navy's Polaris program was also solidly under way at the time of the administration changeover in 1961. The first boat carrying the A-1 version of the Polaris missile was already on station. Firm commitments had been made for about a dozen more. The A-2 and A-3 versions were already being deployed. The A-3, as in the case of the later Minuteman, had a longer range and a larger payload than the first version and was to be supplied with a special new type of warhead known as the Claw.

The Claw consisted of three separate warheads which were launched in such a way that they landed in a tight pattern centering on the aiming point; they were *not* separately targetable. Such a warhead cluster is known as an MRV (multiple reentry vehicles). The reason for the three separate warheads in that case was simply to provide a greater certainty of penetrating an anti–ballistic-missile system such as the Nike-Zeus system, which we had been working on in this country for some time. The Russians had occasionally boasted about knowing how to build an antimissile missile, and our intelligence confirmed that they did have a research and development program in this field.

Secretary McNamara reviewed the Polaris program with

those responsible for it and with the appropriate members of his secretariat. He concluded that the development program and the deployment program should continue along the lines already laid down. He took up the question of how many submarines in all should be built during the sixties and finally settled on a force of forty-one. Secretary Gates had been planning on a force of about forty-five, and the Navy had been urging forty-nine as a minimum.

The range of the A-1 missile was a little over one thousand miles, the range of the A-2 was almost two thousand miles, and the range of the A-3 was almost three thousand miles when fitted with the payload designed for the original version (2,500 miles with a new warhead). The first test flight of the A-3 came in the fall of 1962; the first submarine outfitted with A-3 missiles, the *Daniel Webster,* became operational in the fall of 1964. By the end of 1966, our sea-launched-missile capability consisted of twenty-eight nuclear submarines (SSBNs) armed with A-3s and thirteen armed with A-2s.

Soon after the deployment of the first A-3s, further improvement in the design and the characteristics of solid propellants, inertial-guidance components, and nuclear weapons reached a point where the performance of these submarine-launched ballistic missiles (SLBMs) could be further upgraded. However, since the range of the A-3 was by then long enough for most purposes, these gains were used to improve the warhead and its effectiveness rather than to increase the range. The development of a new weapon system, the Poseidon, was started to exploit these advances in the state of the art. Like the Minuteman III, the Poseidon is scheduled to have a MIRV-type warhead. In discussing this system during the ABM debate in 1969, the Poseidon MIRV warhead was said to consist of ten individually guided warheads of fifty kilotons explosive power each.

This same logical continuation and consolidation of past programs and decisions occurred in the case of other strategic systems.

The Eisenhower Administration had started to cut back the SAGE (Semi-Automatic Ground Environment) air defense system when it was finally appreciated that a precursor attack by ballistic missiles could easily destroy its vital parts and thus allow an almost free passage for any aircraft that might follow afterward. SAGE was further reduced and curtailed during the first years of McNamara's administration.

The Nike-Zeus anti–ballistic-missile system had been carefully reviewed during both the McElroy and Gates administrations. Each time, it had been determined that research and development should continue on a high-priority basis but that the then current design ideas did not merit deployment. McNamara reviewed this matter in the first months of his administration and came to the same conclusion.

We had become disenchanted with the Skybolt air-launched ballistic missile very late in the Eisenhower administration. As a consequence, we deferred indefinitely any firm plans for its deployment and we began to hold back on funding the development program. The new Administration seriously considered canceling the program immediately, but domestic political factors, as well as relations with our British ally, forced the administration to continue the Skybolt for a time. (I heard President Kennedy remark that he needed it to shoot down the B-70.) Even so, a year or so later these political problems had been overcome sufficiently to permit scrubbing this missile.

The old Administration had restored the funds to the B-70 program in late 1960 after virtually canceling the program earlier that same year. The new Administration, after much argument, did succeed in eventually terminating this program also.

The old Administration had also cut back the ANP nuclear-airplane program from a full-scale engine-development program involving a peak annual expenditure rate of almost $200 million to a materials-research and engine-design program which would have involved about $25 million a year. The new Administration gave this program its *coup de grâce*. This same pattern of continuity and consolidation prevailed in other research and development activities, including, specifically, military space applications.

Many persons in Congress, the missile press, the defense industry, and among the public generally had supported Kennedy or at least opposed Eisenhower because they believed that the Eisenhower Administration had done too little too late in responding to what they took to be the threat revealed by Sputnik. Such persons were, to say the least, grossly disappointed by these actions, and their disappointment grew and was greatly aggravated by the failure (as they saw it) to start any "new" weapons systems during the next several years.

To be sure, a few major new (or newish) systems were started, including the TFX, the MIRV, the Poseidon, and the MOL, but these were entirely inadequate for satisfying the demands of the gung-ho types. They felt that the TFX (a joint Air Force–Navy fighter-bomber) was being forced on them by McNamara, and for that reason they never liked it. The MIRV did eventually turn out to have enormous consequences, but it didn't seem too important at the time and, besides, it was not entirely new, being derived from the MRV, which in turn had been started earlier. And the Poseidon not only came along quite late (more than four years after the new Administration took office), but it also looked like nothing more than a fourth version of Polaris that had been given a new name at least partially in response to the charge of "no new weapons systems since 1960." That left the MOL (Manned Orbiting Laboratory), but unfortunately, because of the veil of secrecy surrounding it, the authorities were never able to make its purpose very clear (and it was canceled by Nixon and Laird in 1969).

To make matters worse, by the end of the fifties a great many persons, specifically including high-ranking military officers and many members of the Armed Services Committees of Congress and the Joint Committee on Atomic Energy, had come to believe that the normal technological state of affairs was one of a continuing flow of ever new scientific discoveries automatically leading to ever more exotic applications in turn inevitably producing great new political and strategic advantages for "whoever got there first." The recent past had in fact seen quite an imposing series of developments that were both breakthroughs in the technological sense and highly significant in the political and strategic sense. First came radar, then the A-bomb, then the H-bomb, and then finally the ICBM and the satellites with all their brilliant subtechnologies: propulsion, guidance and control, and reentry. Solid-state electronics had only recently come of age, and the laser had just been invented. As for political significance, radar had played a crucial role in defending Britain in 1940 and 1941, and the A-bomb had ended the war in the Pacific, or so we thought at the time. Today the H-bomb and the ICBM certainly play a very large role in the relations between states having a highly developed technology, even though their relevance in the relationships between two states only one of which has a high level of technology (such as Russia vis-à-vis China, the United States vis-à-vis North Vietnam and North Korea) is not so clear.

The breakthrough, or the "quantum jump," became not only the expected norm, but also the desideratum. Thus, the continuing emphasis throughout the early sixties on the intensive development of older ideas was thought of as being both unimaginative and dangerous. Weapons fanciers in all walks of life not only complained of "no new systems since 1960," some began to yearn for a return to what they came to think of as the lush days of the Eisenhower administration! But not only nontechnical weapons buyers and promoters expected a continuing series of significant breakthroughs and quantum jumps. Many weapons scientists and engineers also believed that such a situation was normal and desirable. They virtually promised their military and Congressional supporters that the future would be as glorious as the recent past, only more so.

Thus, we have Herman Kahn in his book *On Thermonuclear War,* written in 1959 when the rate of breakthroughs seemed to be still rising, making a whole set of extrapolations which turned out to be false. He predicted then that by 1969 we would probably have "cheap simple bombs," "cheap simple missiles," controlled thermonuclear power, "Californium bullets" (by which he meant A-bombs very much smaller than any we now have), and a superior substitute for radar. He said we would be able to put payloads in orbit for only ten dollars a pound. He predicted that by 1973 we would be working on supersonic bombers and supersonic fighters *two generations beyond* the B-70 and the F-108 and that there would be manned offensive satellites and manned defensive satellites in orbit. Every one of these errors in prediction arose out of the twin false assumptions that the immediate past was typical and that the technological future could be predicted by simple extrapolation. These errors are also illustrative of what happens when analysts use sophisticated methods but poor or nonsensical inputs: the final result cannot be better than the inputs no matter how fancily they may be processed. Unfortunately, many technologists as well as laymen don't realize this, and they are repeatedly fooled by the apparent sophistication of efforts like Kahn's 1959 predictions.

A somewhat different example of the same basic error can be found in articles written by Freeman Dyson in 1960 and 1961, during the first nuclear-test moratorium. In essence, he predicted a new, third breakthrough in nuclear weaponry which he appeared to equate with the other two, the A-bomb and the H-bomb. This third type of nuclear weapon was often referred to (rather loosely) as the neutron bomb. Dyson wrote in *Foreign Affairs* in 1960:

> I believe that radically new kinds of nuclear weapons are technically possible, that the military and political effectiveness of such weapons would be im-

portant, and that the development of such bombs can hardly be arrested by any means less drastic than international control of all nuclear operations.

To make it clear that he really meant it when he said they would be militarily and politically important, he presented a little scenario demonstrating what just might happen:

> Imagine a hypothetical situation in which the United States is armed with existing weapons, while some adversary (not necessarily the Soviet Union) has a comparable supply of nuclear fuel and has learned how to ignite it fission free . . . . God help the American infantryman who is sent to fight against such odds. Practically speaking, our army would have only two alternatives, either to retreat precipitously or to strike back with our much more limited number of heavier nuclear weapons and thoroughly destroy the whole country.

A full decade has passed since Dyson wrote his horror tale. To be sure, that's not forever, but there is no sign whatsoever of our precipitously retreating before the threat of such bombs. The question is not so much whether such devices as fission-free or neutron bombs are possible, but whether they are practical and cheap and whether they would really represent a military, let alone a political, breakthrough such as was envisaged even if they were practical. Teller was saying much the same thing at the time, but, most unfortunately and contrary to his own wishes, he was then being kept under wraps on this subject, and so his views were not publicly exposed in any clear way.

I must add, however, that Dyson, unlike the true weapons fancier, did not think the development of such devices would be advantageous to the United States; he just thought they were inevitable. In the *Bulletin of the Atomic Scientists* he wrote in 1961:

> . . . neutron bombs, like hydrogen bombs, will in the long run only complicate our lives, increase our insecurity, and possibly facilitate our extermination. . . . I do not support any of the arguments which have recently appeared in the newspapers claiming that the neutron bomb makes it necessary to resume testing immediately.

I agree very much with his assessment of the situation contained in that last quotation, but the earlier quote is another example of the then very common error of predicting the technology of the future by simply extrapolating the immediate past as if it were typical.

The device which this last argument was about supposedly had an advantage: it could, some said, kill lots of people without damaging much property. It was frequently referred to within the nuclear-weapons trade as the "capitalist bomb," for obvious reasons. Perhaps in this case the bomb can indeed be built. In any event, the important error in the prediction lies in the statements about what its political and strategic significance would be.

As I now see it, there were three good reasons for starting "no new systems" in the early sixties (more correctly, for starting no more than the few that actually were started). Any one of these reasons might have been sufficient.

First, the McNamara administration inherited a number of very large development programs in midstream. These had to be continued and further developed, and they absorbed the bulk of our available resources in terms of good men, money, and facilities. The first Minutemen had an inadequate range (only a little above four thousand nautical miles) and could reach only part of the target area even when sited optimally in this country. During the early sixties, further development work on this missile system extended its range to more than 6,500 miles and produced marked improvements in its accuracy as well as in its ability to penetrate any hypothetical anti-missile defenses. The Polaris went through the same kinds of change. The first Polarises had just been deployed when the new Administration took office in 1961. They had a range of a little over a thousand miles. The submarines carrying them would have had to approach hostile shores very closely, and even then the missile could by no means reach all targets. A set of new developments based on advances in the state of the art pushed the range eventually up to 2,500 miles. This made it possible to reach virtually any target from large parts of the high seas. As in the case of Minuteman, the accuracy of the missile and the means for precisely determining the position of the submarine carrying it were also improved. And for all long-range missiles, including Polaris and Minuteman, intensive research and development programs were necessary to increase their reliability (which turned out to be very much lower than originally anticipated), to enable them to penetrate hypothetical defenses, to cope more adequately with the extremely important problem of command and control, and to assure their survival in the event of an attack on them or, in the case of Polaris, on their carriers.

A rather similar situation prevailed in the cases of other types of weapons systems. Our bombardment aircraft and the equipment they carried, such as missiles and penetration-aid devices, had to be and were further improved. Our antisubmarine devices and techniques had to be improved, and so forth. In short, the intellectual burst of new technological ideas generated by our scientists and engineers in response to the challenge (not the *provocation!*) of the Soviet missile programs (not *Sputnik!*) and of the Soviets' boasts about them had resulted in a large legacy of unfinished business. It had to be properly taken care of before any radically new business could be undertaken.

The *second* inhibiting factor present during the early sixties was a genuine scarcity of new, good technical ideas. Even those few that were generated did not then seem to be relevant to the strategic or political problems at hand or anticipated. Hindsight confirms that, in the strategic-weapons area at least, that view was correct. A number of examples of the kind of idea that was generated in the early sixties and of what was wrong with them could be given, but one will have to suffice here.

Soon after our satellite program got onto a solid footing through the application of the Thor-Agena, Atlas-Agena, and similar space launch vehicles (SLVs in the trade), it was widely realized that no matter how loudly the cry of "Don't put the budget ahead of survival" was made, the cost of orbiting satellites was going to put a real limitation on the use of space as a military arena. By 1961 the cost had dropped to a few thousand dollars per pound in orbit, but, barring the introduction of some entirely different launch methods, there seemed to be little promise of its dropping any further. I should note that the precise total cost depends on how you prorate partial costs such as those involved in development, operation of the missile ranges, recovery when applicable, and other overhead items. But the figure of a few thousand dollars per pound in low earth orbit is adequate for our purposes. On the same basis, it costs almost ten times as much to put satellites in the very high synchronous, or "twenty-four-hour," orbits for communication relay.

Since the smallest manned vehicles weigh a few thousand pounds, and since typical unmanned military satellites as then planned were in the same general weight class, it was clear that the cost per launch could be projected as being $10 million and up. As a result, an intensive search for cheaper ways of launching satellites got under way on a very broad front.

Nearly all governmental organizations and private industries that had programs or responsibilities in any way related to space flight worked on the problem. Some thousands of man years, many of them scrounged from genuinely high-priority programs, were spent on thinking up ideas, transforming them into colorful "airbrushed" sales brochures, and presenting them to an endless series of review boards and Congressional committees. In the process an all too common yet quite improper selling practice was often followed. As part of its sales pitch for a particular program, a company would promise or imply that certain key individuals would carry it out. Then, after winning the bid, the company would put these same people to work on selling yet another idea. One of Admiral Hyman G. Rickover's few positive contributions to defense technology in the sixties was his absolute refusal to countenance this practice in his bailiwick.

Literally, hundreds of millions of dollars of research funds, overhead funds, "bid and quote" funds, were spent on an intensive and widespread effort to find and, above all, to sell solutions to this problem. Practically all of this was government-financed, either directly or through tax deductions.

The many ideas generated may, for simplicity, be divided into two classes. The first class involved launching extremely large single payloads into orbit by one or another more or less exotic means, which even in theory works efficiently only for very large payloads. Various bizarre ideas involving nuclear energy were proposed. One, called Orion, was to be launched into orbit and propelled by a series of hundreds or thousands of individual nuclear explosions. Payloads of thousands of tons were contemplated for this scheme. I am not sure to this day whether the Orion idea was utter nonsense or was simply grossly premature, but for our purposes here it does not matter which. Even if it could be made to work, its hypothetical reduction in launch costs per pound could be realized only in the event of a huge program of interplanetary flight far far beyond anything even now considered relevant or desirable.

The other class of ideas involved using some sort of recoverable booster. Then, as now, the rocket stages used for launching satellites fell into the ocean or onto the tundra and were lost or destroyed after just one use. These stages were, of course, expensive, and so their recovery and reuse could, in principle, result in important cost savings. There were many versions of this recoverable-booster idea, ranging from simply recovering the first stage from the sea, after it had been let down gently by a parachute, to the Aerospace-Plane type of thing which I discussed earlier. In the latter scheme the satellite-launch vehicle was to be flown all the way up into orbit and then back to the ground. Nothing at all was to be lost, discarded, or mutilated. At first blush, such techniques looked as if they might indeed cut launch costs a factor of ten or so. However, in all cases I know about, a thorough examination of the matter—properly prorating development costs, base costs, refurbishing costs and other overhead items—limited potential savings to something well below that figure. And the remaining saving could be realized only in the event of a very much heavier traffic rate than today's space program involves. Even in the case of the anticipated space traffic of the next ten years it has been estimated that the use of recoverable boosters would result in roughly the same cost as the current throwaway-booster technique.

To say it differently and at some risk of too much oversimplification, I estimate that if we spent fifteen times as much as we are spending now per year on our space program (that is, $100 billion) we could launch perhaps one hundred times as much weight into orbit as we are launching now. However, there is no presently known reason for doing so and therefore these new technological schemes cannot yet be effectively used. Thus, although at least some of these new ideas were technologically workable, even these were irrelevant and were not pursued on a full-scale-development basis. Some of them are still being studied and may of course one day be useful, but the decision of McNamara, Webb, Brown, Wiesner and others not to push them in the early sixties was sound.

The *third* factor inhibiting the introduction of new strategic-weapons systems in the early sixties relates to the overkill capability which each of the superpowers possessed by then. Back in the early fifties our strategic forces consisted of medium-range aircraft armed with fission bombs. The numbers and potentials of these weapons were such that they threatened to snuff out the lives of a few million people in a matter of a few hours. By the mid-sixties we had both intercontinental missiles and intercontinental aircraft armed with hydrogen bombs. The numbers and potentials of these weapons were such that we had far more than enough of them to threaten the lives of a few hundred million people in less than an hour. Thus, from the early fifties to the mid-sixties the strategic capabilities of the two superpowers as measured by the amount of destruction they could cause increased about a hundredfold. Whether or not this was desirable or even "thinkable," it certainly was of very great strategic significance, at least insofar as the relations of the two superpowers with each other were concerned. But in achieving this huge "quantum jump" the threat became saturated; that is, large changes in either the numbers or the individual capabilities of the weapons possessed by each side can now produce only small changes in the threat to human life. Only truly extreme changes in weapons capabilities can affect the strategic situation, and hence it is simply *harder* to invent anything that can make a real difference. Thus, horrible as it may otherwise be, this situation of a *saturated* balance of terror does at least lead to a degree of stability.

To be more specific, let us consider a very much simplified version of the strategic situation as of January 1, 1970. At that time, according to our defense officials, the Soviet Union and the United States had very nearly the same number of

ICBMs: about one thousand each. In the case of the United States, fifty-four of these were the large Titan IIs and the rest were Minutemen. For our purposes, we may assume that a Titan II can deliver a single ten-megaton warhead and that a Minuteman can deliver a single one-megaton warhead. In the case of the Soviet Union, some two hundred fifty or so of the ICBMs were the large SS-9s and we may take the rest as being roughly equivalent to the Minuteman. In this case, we may assume that an SS-9 can deliver a twenty-five-megaton warhead and that the other ICBM can deliver a one-megaton warhead. For simplicity, let us also assume that all of these missiles are deployed in silos hard enough to protect them against blast overpressures of up to three hundred pounds per square inch. Finally, let us forget for now all the other strategic weapons that both sides possessed and consider what these ICBM forces alone could do to each other.

We must first note that a twenty-five-megaton bomb exploded on the ground produces three hundred pounds of overpressure per square inch at a distance of about 1.2 miles from the explosion; a ten-megaton explosion produces the same overpressure at about .8 of a mile; a one-megaton explosion, at almost .4 of a mile. But this information is still not enough. In order to calculate precisely what each of these forces could do if fired in a massive surprise attack against the other, we must also know what the accuracy and reliability of each of the various missile systems involved are.

Unfortunately for our immediate goal of making an estimate, no one in authority has revealed specifically just what the accuracy of any of these delivery systems is. There are two reasons for this. First, there is the usual one of security: we don't want to reveal just what the accuracy of our missiles is and we don't want to reveal just how much we know or, possibly, don't know about the accuracy of theirs. The second reason is more fundamental: we really don't know what the accuracy or the reliability of our missiles is, and still less do we know these figures for the Soviet missiles. And the same thing applies the other way around. Of course, we do know something about the reliability of test missiles fired on the test range by test crews under contrived conditions. But these circumstances are quite different from those which would pertain to the operational missiles. And all we can be sure of is that the reliability and the accuracy of the operational missiles are not as good as they are for the test missiles. The same lack of knowledge applies in the case of silo hardness: we really don't know how close a hit by, say, a one-megaton bomb our silos could withstand, and we don't know what it really takes to destroy one of theirs.

Thus, no one really knows the figures that are necessary in order to make a precise calculation of what one of these forces could do against the others. And anyone who pretends to present such exact figures is indulging in a kind of useless and potentially harmful mathematical nonsense. However, *crude* estimates can be sensibly made. These, I believe, indicate that, roughly speaking, each time the button is pressed for launching a missile carrying a one-megaton weapon, there is less than a fifty-fifty chance that an enemy missile in a hard silo will be destroyed, and each time the button is pressed for launching one of the bigger weapons that each side possesses, there is somewhat more than a fifty-fifty chance. In the often strange jargon of strategic analysis, these odds are referred to as "kill probabilities" whether or not human life is directly involved. What this means, then, is that well over half of the missile forces each side possessed at the very beginning of the seventies would have survived a massive surprise attack by the other side's missile forces under the assumed set of circumstances.

Most professional analysts of the subject believe that the prospect of about one hundred thermonuclear warheads exploding over urban areas is more than enough to deter either side from starting a nuclear war. Therefore the more than five hundred missiles that would have survived the surprise attack we postulated would be very much more than sufficient for deterrence.

I personally believe that very much smaller numbers are sufficient to deter war; I have used numbers like one hundred only because it is customary to do so in such arguments, and because the above arguments do not hinge on whether the number is in fact one hundred or something very much smaller. In this regard, McGeorge Bundy, who had been Special Assistant for National Security Affairs to both President Kennedy and President Johnson, recently wrote in *Foreign Affairs:*

> In the real world of real political leaders—whether here or in the Soviet Union—a decision that would bring even one hydrogen bomb on one city of one's own country would be recognized in advance as a catastrophic blunder; ten bombs on ten cities would be a disaster beyond history; and a hundred bombs on a hundred cities are unthinkable.

Amen.

But to continue with the ideas and in the language of those whose profession is analyzing strategy: Each side could be confident of retaining an "assured destruction capability" after a surprise attack by the other. Therefore each side possessed a "credible deterrent" to a "preemptive attack" by the other.

To put this whole matter the other way around, neither side could have had any confidence whatsoever that by making a surprise preemptive attack it could reduce the other side's retaliatory capability to an acceptable level. This last way of looking at the question is the one that really counts. The surprise attacker by definition has the initiative, and accordingly it is *his* view of the situation that determines whether or not something will happen and thus whether or not the defender possesses a "credible deterrent."

A complete analysis of this matter would require considering the bombers and the Polaris missiles also, but the land-based missiles are commonly considered to be the single most important element of the deterrent, and including these others would not substantially change the preceding analysis. Nor would this situation have been changed substantially even if one side had, say, twice as many missiles as the other. As long as the mix of types and their characteristics were not radically changed, the attacker would still not have been able to be confident of reducing the other side's forces below the number that could wreak an unacceptable revenge. Thus the situation at the beginning of the seventies was one of stability and strategic parity. Even considering silo-based missile forces alone, each side possessed many more missiles than were necessary for deterrence, and neither side possessed nearly enough missiles to risk a preemptive strike.

Thus a balance of terror had been created such that neither side could conceivably survive a nuclear exchange no matter who struck first, and even fairly large deviations from strict numerical parity could not seriously upset the balance.

PART TWO

Unbalancing the Balance of Terror

9

MIRV:
THE MULTIPLE MENACE

As the decade of the seventies begins, four technological advances threaten to upset the strategic stability, or balance of terror, that I described in the last chapter. These are (1) improvements in reliability, (2) further improvements in guidance accuracy, (3) MIRV, and (4) ABM.

Now, as in the recent past, accuracy is the factor that has the strongest effect on the probability of destroying a hard target. But the accuracies now in prospect are so good that missile reliability may become most important. In many cases, the kill probability, if everything works as it should, will be so close to one hundred percent that the probability of everything working as it should can become the dominant factor in determining the net kill probability. The measure of whether or not everything works as it should is the "reliability" of the system. This reliability is not known for operational missiles under operational conditions, it is known only for test missiles under test conditions. Dr. Daniel Fink, who had been Deputy Director of Defense Research and Engineering under both Harold Brown and his successor, John S. Foster, Jr., estimated it at forty percent to sixty-five percent. Improving this figure is largely a matter of procedures such as quality-control methods. If basic changes in the system design are held to a minimum, thus avoiding new "bugs," it is reasonable to suppose that ultimately this figure will improve somewhat. Also, those failures that occur early in missile flight can in principle be observed early enough so that the failed missile can be immediately replaced by another. This method of early replacement works in theory if the over-all reliability is not too low and if nearly all failures do indeed occur early in flight.

However, doing this in practice during a huge massive attack with perhaps a thousand missiles and many thousand warheads in the air simultaneously is quite another matter. For one thing, an experimental check of the technique at full scale is impossible. However, during the 1969 ABM debates, Foster and Albert Wohlstetter, one of the sounder ABM supporters from outside the government, both implied that the Soviets would (or could) have a combination of intrinsic reliability plus an early-replacement capability such that the equivalent reliability would be practically one hundred percent. I very much doubt that this will be true in the real world in the mid-seventies, but if Foster and Wohlstetter can think so, then others with authority and influence can think so, too. And on this question of the stability of the deterrent, what such people think has as much effect as does reality.

The second technological advance that threatens to upset the current strategic stability is further improvement in guidance technology. Accuracy is measured in terms of CEP, the circular error probable. This CEP is the distance from the aiming point within which one half of a large number of otherwise similar shots would fall. To get a feeling for the significance of accuracy, we may note that a one-megaton weapon with a CEP of half a nautical mile fired against a target hardened to survive a blast overpressure of three hundred pounds per square inch would have a kill probability of thirty-two percent. If the CEP were reduced to a quarter of a mile, the kill probability would be about seventy-eight percent, and for an eighth of a mile it would be essentially one hundred percent.

The following table shows how these "kill probabilities" vary with accuracy for warheads of other strengths. We can see that for accuracies of a quarter of a mile or worse (the present situation) only "big" bombs (one megaton and up) have high kill probabilities when used against missiles stored in very hard silos. But for accuracies of an eighth of a mile (coming) all sizes of bombs considered, even the so-called "small" MIRV warheads carried by the Poseidon, have high kill probabilities.

"KILL PROBABILITY" VERSUS ACCURACY (CEP) FOR VARIOUS WARHEAD YIELDS

(300-p.s.i.* hard target and 100% reliability are assumed)

Missile	Warhead Type	Yield	CEP: ½ mile	CEP: ¼ mile	CEP: ⅛ mile
Poseidon (U.S.)	MIRV	50 KT	5%	19%	56%
Minuteman (U.S.)	MIRV	200 KT	12	40	87
Minuteman (U.S.) / SS-11 (U.S.S.R.)	single	1 MT	32	78	100
SS-9 (U.S.S.R.)	MIRV	5 MT	68	99	100

* Per square inch.

The third item on a list of technological advances that threatens to destabilize things is MIRV.

MIRV was one of the few new weapons systems started in the early sixties. It has had a much more profound effect on the strategic situation and on the arms race than was anticipated at its beginning. It has been so much discussed and debated both in public and in private that the letters "MIRV" have come to be accepted as a word that can be declined as a noun or conjugated as a verb.

The origin of the concept of multiple independently targetable reentry vehicles can be usefully traced back to 1958. By that time we had already spent many millions for research on and development of various concepts for defense against missiles. One ABM, our anti–ballistic-missile, the Army's Nike-Zeus, had reached such a stage in its development that it began to appear possible to intercept simple large warheads of the type then intended for our offensive missiles. Also, about the same time, our intelligence agencies confirmed the existence of an already large and still growing ABM development program in the Soviet Union. And Khrushchev in his own inimitable way had boasted of Soviet capabilities-to-come in this type of weaponry. With all this in the background, the designers and promoters of ballistic-missiles systems began to take the challenge of the *anti*–ballistic-missile seriously. In a relatively short time they considered a great many ideas, inventions, and tactics designed to enable ballistic-missile warheads to penetrate any ABM defense then known. Collectively, these are known as penetration aids. The most important insofar as the then unforeseen consequences were concerned was the notion of putting more than one warhead on each launch vehicle. At first this last idea simply involved a "shotgun" technique in which the several warheads landed in a tight pattern around the aiming point. But of course almost immediately it was proposed that each of these be separately aimed and targeted.

It is this last refinement that we now call MIRV.

Several programs to explore these ideas and then develop the better ones further were initiated almost right away. One of these had as its objective the development of the threefold

Claw warhead for the A-3 version of the Polaris. It seemed especially important to provide Polaris with this multiple-reentry-vehicle capability, since at that time there didn't seem to be any other good way of gaining the type of advantage for the offense that is provided by a barrage of simultaneously arriving warheads. The Claw was to be of the "shotgun" type, however, since the techniques for independently targeting the individual warhead had not yet been worked out adequately. As time went on, the designers of the defense began to invent methods for discriminating decoys from warheads and for coping with jammers and chaff. In my mind there has always been and still remains very considerable doubt about the true efficacy of such discrimination techniques. However, the possibility of their coming into being ultimately pushed the designers of the offense into placing greatest emphasis on multiple warheads as the one sure way of making the defending ABM fire at every incoming object. Thus the defense would be overpowered by simple exhaustion even if no other penetration aids or tactics worked.

A favorite MIRV design nowadays involves launching an object called a "bus" onto a normal missile trajectory. This bus carries on board all the various individual warheads. It is equipped with its own inertial-guidance system and it is provided with a set of small motors that can be used to change its orientation, direction, and velocity. When the bus is properly aimed at the first of a series of programmed targets, it very gently drops off its first warhead. This warhead then continues on the same course toward target number one. Next, the guidance system and the rocket motors modify the velocity and direction of the bus so that it is aimed at a second target. It then gently drops off its second warhead to proceed inexorably to target number two. The same maneuver is repeated again and again until it has aimed each of its passengers toward a separate preselected target.

We have already seen that without MIRV, and with only

approximately numerically equal forces on each side, neither side can hope to "wipe out" the other in a surprise attack. Because of missiles that fail and warheads that miss, a significant number of missiles will always survive the attack. Even if the two forces are somewhat out of numerical balance, uncertainties in the estimates of how effective an attack would be will still very powerfully inhibit even the side that possesses the numerically superior force. Further, if one side does start to get too far ahead in numbers (say, one side has more than double what the other has) the other side can in principle bring things back onto an even keel by proliferating his forces, and other drastic but effective means, such as the dreadful launch-on-warning technique which I will discuss later, can be employed if necessary during the time it takes to readjust the numerical balance.

MIRV completely eliminates even the possibility of this sort of balance. MIRV makes it easily possible for *each* side to have many more warheads than the *other* side has missiles. With presently planned warhead multiplicities, and with foreseeable accuracies and reliabilities, each side will eventually be able to wipe out better than ninety-five percent of the other side's silo-based missile force in a surprise attack. The possibility of the Soviets' achieving such a capability against us in the mid-seventies was one of the reasons given by the Nixon Administration in 1969 for proposing deployment of the Safeguard ABM system. Indeed, the question is when, not whether, this can happen. We will come back to this matter later; for now, suffice it to say that I believe this time will not come before 1980, and that in any event the Safeguard ABM is an inappropriate solution to the genuinely serious problem that will be created when one or both of us achieves this capability in his *operational* forces.

The fourth item on the list of technological developments that threatens to destabilize the present balance of terror is the development of the ABM. We will discuss the technical aspects and possibilities of that type of system in a separate chapter. Here we need note only the arguments usually presented by strategic analysts about how the ABM can influence stability. According to such analyses, if an ABM system is deployed so as to protect the population generally, it will add to the instability brought about by MIRV. The reason is that even after a surprise attack by MIRVed forces (as described just above) there will still be some residual forces left for retaliation. But these will be numerically small, and a population defense, even though inevitably imperfect, might be able to intercept enough of them to reduce the expected casualties to what these theorists refer to as an "acceptable" level. In this view, MIRV plus population defense make preemption look more promising than MIRV alone. Hence their combination is destabilizing.

On the other hand, an ABM system in which the defender could have very high confidence, and which was used to defend his deterrent (the ostensible purpose of Safeguard), should be stabilizing by virtue of increasing the anticipated retaliation that would follow a surprise attack.

I believe these analyses are correct in an abstract sense; however, I heavily discount their relevance in the real world. It's not all that easy to distinguish between population defense and deterrent defense, especially at an early phase of deployment. Also, this kind of highly convoluted argument, even if correct, does not carry nearly as much weight among ruling politicians as it does among theoreticians. In my view, the main reason an ABM program (any ABM program I have heard of) is dangerous and destabilizing is that it is simply another step in the arms race. It presents a technical challenge (again, not a political provocation!) to the technologists who design the offense. In designing around the ABM, these latter will usually come up with a more complex, more expensive, more deadly and more volatile offense. Our ultimate response to the Soviet ABM was MIRV. If current plans continue, fewer than one hundred Soviet ABM missiles now deployed around

Moscow will have resulted before very long in an increase in the number of U. S. warheads by more than five thousand. *Thus, as a matter of historical fact, the Soviet ABM program has been fantastically counterproductive and has had anything but a stabilizing effect.*

This sequence of steps did not come about as a result of careful analyses of the political significance of each preceding step and considerations of such matter as stability. The technologists on each side took what the other side was doing as a challenge; they designed new systems to counter the challenge, they sold these to the officials and politicians in charge, and then sometimes they performed careful after-the-fact analyses that rationalized the whole thing when it was already too late to do anything about it. The technological side of the arms race has a life of its own, almost independent of policy and politics. McNamara himself described this situation in his famous San Francisco speech (1967) by saying, "There is a kind of mad momentum intrinsic to the development of all nuclear weaponry. If a system works—and works well—there is a strong pressure from all directions to procure and deploy the weapon out of all proportion to the prudent level required."

Let us return to a more detailed look at MIRV and its political meaning. Some American analysts have said that the U. S. MIRV program is very different from the Soviet MIRV program insofar as the threat to the stability of the present strategic-arms balance is concerned. I believe this supposed asymmetry exists only in the eye of the beholder. U.S. analysts know about all the little nitty-gritty problems that have beset our programs, and in the interest of "erring on the side of military safety" they downgrade (often unconsciously) the capability of our missiles. These same people, when they look at the Soviet system, are largely unaware of the myriad small problems that add up to big difficulties in the real Soviet Union. They emphasize "the worst plausible case," which in this situation means making almost mystic assumptions about

Soviet technology, and they (again often unconsciously) upgrade the capability of Soviet missiles.

Let us consider the American MIRV as it might be viewed by a Soviet analyst. Suppose the entire Minuteman force is converted to the Minuteman III with a MIRV warhead consisting of three 200-kiloton individual warheads. If each of these has a one-quarter-mile CEP, then each one of them, if successfully launched, would have a forty percent chance of destroying a Soviet missile in its silo. If all three are launched at the same silo, the kill probability goes up to almost eighty percent.

Real reliabilities reduce the net "kill probability" further, and the resulting figure is not enough to make a preemptive attack "interesting" in the case of a one-quarter-mile CEP. But what about a one-eighth-mile CEP? Under such conditions, only two of the three Minuteman MIRV warheads are needed to achieve well over ninety-eight percent kill probability, leaving the third warhead for use either as a replacement for other missiles that failed at or near launch or for other purposes. And is a one-eighth-mile CEP so improbable? We have improved our CEPs almost twentyfold in the sixteen years since we started our ICBM development program. Another factor of two does not look very large by comparison. And the accuracy requirement set for our first ICBM, the Atlas, was just twenty times the accuracy actually achieved by the V-2 only ten years before that. The net improvement in twenty-five years has been four-hundredfold! Furthermore, there are no fundamental laws forbidding still further improvements, and eventually we will no doubt go well below one eighth of a mile. Even the so-called "small" fifty-kiloton warhead postulated for the Poseidon MIRV will be quite effective at destroying silo-based missiles when this system achieves a one-eighth-mile CEP. A single shot with such a missile would result in a kill probability of about fifty-six percent. This means that only four shots at the same target would result in about a ninety-six percent net probability of destruction, and each Poseidon MIRV will have ten such warheads!

The U. S. missile force with the planned MIRV modification and a perfectly plausible extrapolation of *our* present accuracy is every bit as suitable for a preemptive attack as is the Soviets' missile force after MIRVing and with what we take to be a plausible extrapolation of *their* present accuracy (which, generally, has been behind ours). It is easy to imagine that in times of tension such a situation would be fraught with danger. *Each side, believing the other could make a preemptive attack, would certainly be stimulated to consider doing so first.*

Of course, the situation described above differs from reality in one essential respect. It ignores the fact that there are other components to the deterrent besides the silo-based missiles. The MIRV–accuracy–yield–numbers combination assumed above does not similarly threaten either our missile submarine force or our bomber force, since these are protected against surprise attack by other means. The submarine force is protected simply by being hidden in the murky seas, and the bombers are protected by being normally placed on an alert status such that a substantial fraction of them could become airborne in the warning time that can be anticipated.

However, even having just one component of our deterrent become so vulnerable to a preemptive attack is bound to cause concern. It is always possible to imagine that somehow something parallel may happen to the other components and then we really might be in a fix. I regard this simultaneous vulnerability of all components of our strategic forces as being completely incredible, but, even so, it is prudent to think about what should and could be done to avoid a situation in which even one major component of our strategic forces becomes vulnerable to a preemptive strike.

Many ideas for protecting our land-based missile forces against a reliable and accurate MIRV attack have been suggested and studied. In my judgment, all save one are inadequate from a technological point of view, and that one is unacceptable for other reasons. The inadequate solutions include superhardening, the "Safeguard" ABM system, proliferation, a "shell game" in which there are more silos than missiles, and land-mobile missiles. Although I was personally hopeful before the 1969 ABM hearings that at least one of these approaches would maintain its invulnerability, a review of those debates leaves me now with the pessimistic view that none of them holds much promise beyond the next ten years.

Silo-hardening most probably does work now, in the sense that the combination of SS-11 accuracy and yield and Minuteman silo-hardening works out in such a way that one incoming warhead (and hence one SS-11 missile) has less than a fifty-fifty chance of destroying a Minuteman. If, however, one considers the technological trends in hardening, yield per unit weight, MIRVing, and accuracy, it does seem convincing that this is a game that the offense eventually will win. Albert Wohlstetter, testifying in favor of the Safeguard system before the Senate Armed Services Committee, quoted a paper he wrote with Fred Hoffman in 1954 (long before any ICBMs were actually in place anywhere) predicting that the ability of silo-hardening to protect offensive missiles would run out by the end of the 1960s. This remarkably prescient study is wrong only in numerical detail. If we take the same rosy view of technology that was taken in almost all the pro-ABM arguments, then hardening will not work for more than another five years. My own view of the technological future is clearly much less rosy, but I do believe that the situation in which hardening is no longer the answer could come by, say, 1980 or, more appropriately, 1984.

Protection of a land-based ICBM by an ABM system also appears to me to be quite inadequate as a means for reestablishing a high level of confidence in the assured survival of this component of the deterrent. The Safeguard ABM as originally

184 UNBALANCING THE BALANCE OF TERROR

proposed would be too weak and thin to provide protection against a determined enemy; an ABM which would provide an effective shield would in my opinion cost vastly more than we would be willing to pay. The same thing applies to the Soviets. I will have more to say about this in the next chapter.

Proliferation of Minuteman would have worked in the absence of MIRV. Now, however, it would seem that the ability to MIRV, which no doubt can eventually be carried much further than the fewfold MIRV we see for the immediate future, clearly makes proliferation a losing game as well as the dangerous one it always was.

The "shell game" has not, in my view, been analyzed in satisfactory detail, but it would appear to have a serious destabilizing effect on the arms race. Schemes have been suggested for verifying that a certain fraction of the missile holes are in fact empty, but one can foresee a growing and persistent belief on each side that the "other missiles" must be hidden somewhere.

Road-mobile and rail-mobile versions of Minuteman have been seriously studied for well over a decade. These ideas have always foundered on two basic difficulties: (1) such systems are inherently soft and hence can be attacked by very large warheads without precise knowledge of where they are, and (2) railroads and highways all pass through population centers, and large political and social problems seem unavoidable. Off-road systems have been considered, too, but they suffer from severe geographic restrictions.

Where does all this leave us? Can we find a technical solution for protecting Minuteman? Is a balance of terror possible with MIRVs in the strategic forces? One and only one technically viable solution seems to have emerged for the long run: launch on warning. Such an idea has been considered seriously by some politicians, some technical men, and some military officers.

In theory, launch on warning could be managed entirely

by automatic devices or the command and control system could be such as to require authorization to launch by some very high human authority.

In the case of the first alternative, people who think about such things envision a system consisting of probably two types of detection device that could, in principle, determine if a massive launch had been made and then, somewhat later, determine that such a launch consisted of multiple warheads aimed at our missile-silo fields. This information would be processed by a computer which would then launch the Minutemen so that the incoming missiles would find only empty holes; consequently the Minutemen would be able to carry out their mission of revenge. Thus, the steady advance of arms technology may be leading us not to the ultimate weapon but rather to the ultimate absurdity: a completely automatic system for deciding whether or not doomsday has arrived.

To me, such an approach to the problem is politically and morally unacceptable, and if it really is the only approach, then clearly we have been considering the wrong problem. Instead of asking how Minuteman can be protected, we should be asking what the alternatives to Minuteman are. And, much more important, instead of blithely moving toward a balance of terror of a still more gruesome and precarious sort, we should be asking what the alternatives to a balance of terror might be.

Evidently most other people also find the launch-on-warning idea unacceptable once they think about it. The Army found it necessary to reassure people repeatedly that ABM missiles would not be launched without the approval of "the highest authorities," even though this is clearly a far less serious matter in the case of the ABM missiles than in the case of Minuteman.

The theoretical alternative is to require that a human decision-maker at the level of "the highest authorities" be introduced into the decision-making loop. But is this really satisfactory? We would be asking that a human being make in just a few minutes a decision to utterly destroy another country. (After all, there would be no point in firing at their empty silos.) If, for any reason whatever, he were responding to a false alarm or to some kind of smaller, perhaps "accidental," attack, he would be ensuring that a massive deliberate attack on us would take place moments later. Considering the shortness of the time, the complexity of the information and the awesomeness of the moment, the President would himself have to be properly preprogrammed in order to make such a decision.

Those who argue that the command and control system is perfect or perfectable forget that human beings are not. If forced to choose, I would prefer a preprogrammed President to a computer when it came to deciding whether or not doomsday had arrived, but again I feel that this solution too is really unacceptable, and that once again, in attempting to defend Minuteman, we are simply dealing with the wrong problem. For the present it would seem that the Polarises and the bombers are not, as systems, subject to the same objections, since there are now enough other approaches to the problem of ensuring their invulnerability to sudden massive destruction.

It is important to realize that this launch-on-warning idea neither is new nor has been casually offered. Back in the fifties when the design requirement for being able to launch the large liquid-fueled ICBMs in fifteen minutes or less was first established, it was precisely this capability of being able to launch the missile on warning that determined this time interval. The warning time available from radars located on the fringes of the continent would be fifteen to twenty minutes. Newer technology—over-the-horizon radars and satellites—can in principle observe the launching itself and hence provide thirty minutes of warning, or about twice the launch-time requirement established back in the fifties. Also, one of the main reasons for substituting the smaller solid-propellant Minuteman for the larger liquid-propellant Atlases and Titans as the main component of our deterrent forces was that this missile could be launched in an even shorter time. Its name implies that it can be launched in about one minute after receipt of warning.

In 1960 I paid an official visit to the North American Air Defense Command headquarters in Colorado Springs. Among other things, the commander told me that a further expansion in our ballistic-missile early-warning system (BMEWS) was urgently needed so as to reduce the probability of a false alarm resulting in the launching of our ICBMs. It was clear from the conversation that he had in mind minimum human intervention in the electronic network which would connect the warning system to the launch-control circuits, or "the button," as it is often called. I replied to the effect that I felt our warning system was never likely to reach a state of such absolute reliability that we could be willing to risk launch on warning, especially if no outside higher-level human intervention was allowed. The commander and some of the other general officers present were obviously appalled by my lack of confidence in the potentialities of technology, and one of them said to me quite literally, "Well, in that case, we might as well surrender now."

Before MIRV, we could fight off such nonsense by simply pointing out that, in a careful analysis, it wasn't necessary. Now, with MIRV, and with further advances in reliability and accuracy in prospect, we are being forced to consider these horrors again. The only possible conclusion is that it is the arms race as a whole, and not just some of its details, that is rapidly and inexorably diminishing our national security.

10

THE DEFENSE DELUSION

One of the most misleading aspects of the arms race is the notion of defense. The technical dynamics of nuclear strategy have blurred many of the distinctions between offensive and defensive weapons. A great irony of the arms race is that measures taken ostensibly for defensive purposes can seem to the enemy as great a threat as or perhaps even a greater threat than avowedly offensive measures. In this situation, defensive programs such as the air defense system and the ABM have contributed as much as anything else to intensifying arms competition.

By 1960, the United States had spent more than $20 billion on a continental air defense system. The over-all system consisted of many separate components for detecting, tracking, and intercepting incoming bombers.

The northernmost part of the detection and tracking system was known as the DEW line (distant early-warning). It consisted of a line of radars located in Alaska and Canada, with naval vessels providing seaward extensions on both ends. Other radars were located farther south in Canada and within the United States itself. The interceptors included a variety of aircraft, a cruise missile (the Air Force's Bomarc) and two short-range ballistic missiles (the Army's Nike-Ajax and Nike-Hercules). Each of these interceptors required its own special command and control system for getting it to the appropriate point in space at the right time to intercept or "kill" the attacking bomber. These individual command and control systems consisted of additional radars, computers, and special communications networks.

Clearly, such a complex system, consisting as it did of so many different components, would work better if the whole thing were tied together and operated as a unit. A system for doing so was designed and developed during the fifties; it was called SAGE, for Semi-Automatic Ground Environment. SAGE was to consist of about a dozen command centers located around the periphery of the United States. Each of them was to be equipped with a computer suitable for directing and coordinating the entire air defense battle in its zone. Data from the various lines of radar detectors were to be fed into the appropriate computers. The computers were to decide which of the various interceptors would be assigned to a particular attacker, and the necessary orders and detailed instructions for making the intercept were to be sent out to the weapons in the field. These peripheral command centers were in turn to be tied in to one central command post located in Colorado Springs, headquarters of NORAD, the North American Air Defense Command. The name SAGE eventually came to be commonly used to describe the over-all continental air defense system.

As time went on, it turned out to be harder to design such a system than had been anticipated. Serious doubts arose about the ability of the system to cope with the threat as originally perceived. The usual programmatic delays resulted, and before SAGE could be placed in operation ICBMs passed from theory to reality.

The whole matter of continental defense had to be restudied. SAGE was found to be totally vulnerable to a combined bomber and missile attack. It became painfully evident that SAGE would be obsolete before it could be operating. At the same time, technical difficulties were experienced in the development of other components of the over-all continental air defense system, and unanticipated political problems arose over the deployment of nuclear armed interceptors in Canada. Together these factors in 1959 resulted in a substantial cutback in our plans for the deployment of both SAGE and the associated weapons systems. Further cutbacks were made in the first years of the Kennedy administration. As a result, the air defense system we now have is only a shadow of what we once had in mind. Even so, we spent over $1 billion a year on it during the sixties.

Each of the individual components of this over-all system works quite well in the test-range sense. That is, on a missile test range test crews can detect a suitable drone target with their radars and can then intercept and destroy it with a Bomarc or Nike-Hercules or other weapon. Even so, experts generally agree that the present over-all system would not produce any important level of attrition in the event of a real attack on it. Nor would the original system be capable of doing so had it been built.

The same conclusions apply to the attempts of the U.S.S.R. to build an air defense. The Russians have always been more defense-minded than we have. As a result, not only have they spent a greater fraction of their strategic-arms budget on defense systems, they have invested much more money in defensive systems even on an absolute basis. The best estimates say that the Soviets have spent to date (1970) about $75 billion, in contrast to our $30 billion. Even so, our Strategic Air Command believes that it can penetrate Soviet air defenses with a sufficiently high probability to carry out its mission. Almost all independent authorities agree with this estimate.

The problem of air defense is entirely different in the nuclear age from what it was before. In World War II the damage from the amount of chemical high explosives that a bomber could carry on one trip was so small that very many repetitive trips had to be made by each bomber and each crew in order to attain a significant total level of damage. An attrition rate of only ten percent or so by the defenses was sufficient to prevent the necessary number of repetitive strikes or sorties. Now the damage that a single bomber armed with a hydrogen bomb can do is so enormous that an attrition of ninety percent, allowing a penetration of only ten percent, is wholly inadequate as a defense. For example, a "mere" ten percent of our SAC bomber forces alone could deliver *more than a hundred thousand times* as much explosive power as killed those one hundred thousand human beings in Hiroshima.

The Soviet air defense equipment deployed in North Vietnam during the late sixties was not able to achieve anything like the ten percent necessary for effective defense against bombers carrying chemical explosives. The home defenses of the U.S.S.R. are, of course, much more extensive and consist of more modern and advanced types of equipment than the surface-to-air missiles (SAM) and antiaircraft artillery deployed in North Vietnam. However, I know of no estimate that says they could achieve the ninety-five-percent-plus level of attrition necessary against a massive sophisticated nuclear attack. On the contrary, estimates by persons in whom I have confidence range from pessimistic (for us) estimates of forty percent attrition of our SAC bombers by Soviet air defenses down to more optimistic estimates of only ten percent attrition. My personal view is that the optimists are probably more nearly right in this case.

If we have not bought an effective air defense for our $30 billion and they have not bought an effective air defense for their $75 billion, what have we each done? One answer is that each of us has prevented the other from having a free ride. That is, if we had no air defense, then presumably they could attack us with simple and cheap bombers, and vice versa. This is not strictly true, however, since the need for speed and great range would still be there even in the absence of any defense, and, furthermore, the possibility of at least some modest defense capability would have to be anticipated. But, even so, their air defense has forced us to spend much more money on our bomber fleet than we otherwise would have. We have bought many more aircraft and each one is more expensive because of the demand for high performance and the need to provide it with various kinds of penetration aids such as radar jammers and chaff. We must suppose the same has been true for the Soviets. Thus, one result of air defenses has been to induce each side to spend more money on bombers.

But that isn't all. The possibility of successful defense against bombers was one of the principal driving forces behind the development of missiles. Anyone who took seriously the articles and especially the advertisements in the missile press during the fifties could only conclude that not even a fly could penetrate the borders of the United States without proper clearance. Ballistic-missile warheads, with their greater speed and smaller size, then as now appeared to be much less vulnerable than bombers to defensive measures and hence more certain of being able to deliver their payload to their assigned targets. There were, of course, other rationales and arguments for the development of long-range ballistic missiles, but leapfrogging defensive technology was perhaps the most important on both sides.

Thus, the net result of the development and deployment of bomber defenses by each of the superpowers has been to force the other to increase greatly the number of individual weapons in its offensive forces and to multiply the number of different kinds of forces making up its strategic offense. We have here before us another simple, clear example of how it is that purely defensive weapons accelerate the arms race and how it is that each turn around the arms-race spiral ends up with more human lives at risk than before. In the mad logic of the arms race, bombers led inexorably to bomber defenses, and these in turn led to fancier, more complex, and more deadly bombers as well as to entirely new kinds of offense, the intercontinental ballistic missile and the submarine-launched ballistic missile.

It became evident, in the early fifties, that the state of the art of nuclear weaponry, rocket propulsion, and missile guidance and control had reached the point in the U. S. where a strategically useful ICBM could be built. At about the same time, the fact that a major long-range-missile development program was in progress in the U.S.S.R. was confirmed. As a result of the confluence of these two events the tremendous U. S. long-range-missile program, which dominated the technological scene for more than a decade, was undertaken.

Also at about the same time, the Army, which had had the responsibility for ground-based air defense (including the Nike-Ajax and Nike-Hercules surface-to-air missiles, or SAMs), began to study the problem of how to intercept ICBMs, and soon afterward (in 1956) it initiated the Nike-Zeus program. This program was a straightforward attempt to use existing technology in the design of a nuclear-armed rocket for the purpose of intercepting a single uncomplicated incoming warhead. The Air Force, as is its style, proposed more exotic solutions to the missile-defense problem, but these were subsequently either dropped or absorbed into the Defender program of the Department of Defense's Advanced Research Projects Agency (ARPA). The Defender program included the study of designs more advanced than Nike-Zeus, and it also incorporated a program of down-range measurements designed to find out what really went on during the terminal phases of missile flight.

By 1960, indications that the Russians were taking the ABM prospect seriously, in addition to progress in our own Nike-Zeus program, stimulated the designers of our offensive missiles into seriously studying the problem of how to penetrate missile defenses. Very quickly a host of "penetration-aid" concepts came to light: light and heavy decoys, including balloons, tank fragments and objects resembling children's jacks; electronic countermeasures, including radar-reflecting clouds of the small wires called chaff; radar blackout by means of high-altitude nuclear explosions; tactics such as barrage, local exhaustion and "rollback" of the defense; and MRV (Multiple Reentry Vehicles). These last were good only against large-area targets (cities), but MRV soon developed into MIRV (Multiple Independent Reentry Vehicles), which eventually will be useful against smaller, harder targets such as missile silos, radars and command centers.

This avalanche of concepts forced the ABM designers to go back to the drawing board, and as a result the Nike-X concept was born in 1962. The Nike-X designers attempted to make use of the more sophisticated and up-to-date technology developed under the Defender program in the design of a system that they hoped might be able to cope with a large, sophisticated attack. All through the mid-1960s a vigorous battle of defensive concepts and designs versus offensive concepts and designs took place. This battle was waged partly on the Atlantic and Pacific missile ranges but mostly on paper and in committee meetings. It took place generally in secret, although parts of it were discussed in the open literature and before Congressional committees.

This intellectual battle culminated in a meeting that took place in the White House in January, 1967. In addition to President Johnson, Secretary of Defense Robert S. McNamara and the Joint Chiefs of Staff, there were present all past and current Special Assistants to the President for Science and Technology (James R. Killian, Jr., George B. Kistiakowsky, Jerome B. Wiesner and Donald F. Hornig) and all past and current Directors of Defense Research and Engineering (Harold Brown, John S. Foster, Jr., and myself). We were asked that simple kind of question which must be answered after all the complicated ifs, ands and buts have been discussed: "Will it work and should it be deployed?" The answer in relation to defending our people against a Soviet missile attack was

No, and there was no dissent from that answer. The context, of course, was the Russian threat as it was then interpreted and forecast, and the current and projected state of our ABM technology. There was also some discussion of this same question in relation to a hypothetical Red Chinese missile threat. In this latter case, there was some divergence of views, although the majority view (and my own) was still No.

Later that year, Secretary McNamara gave his famous San Francisco speech in which he reiterated his belief that we could not build an ABM system capable of protecting us from destruction in the event of a Russian attack. He did state, however, that the decision had been made (I presume by the President) to build an ABM system able to cope with a hypothetical Chinese missile attack, which by definition would be "light" and uncomplicated. In announcing that we would go ahead with a program to build what came to be known as the Sentinel system, he said, "There are marginal grounds for concluding that a light deployment of U. S. ABMs against this probability is prudent." A few sentences later, however, he warned, "The danger in deploying this relatively light and reliable Chinese-oriented ABM system is going to be that pressures will develop to expand it into a heavy Soviet-oriented ABM system." The record makes it clear that he was quite right in this prediction.

The Congress, in the course of authorizing and appropriating funds for fiscal year 1969 (beginning July 1, 1968), approved deployment of the Sentinel system without much debate, and soon afterward the Army started to acquire property for use as missile sites near Boston, Chicago, and Seattle. It sent teams out to those areas to win local support, but instead the citizenry became alarmed and began to object strenuously to having their neighborhoods turned into what they thought would be prime targets. Many people wrote their Representatives and Senators about their views, and some of these in turn began to give more serious attention to the whole matter.

Meanwhile, Richard Nixon was elected and inaugurated

President of the United States. Some of his technical advisers had for some time strongly favored deploying an ABM system, but an ABM system of a different sort and for reasons different from those used to justify Sentinel. They held that defending our deterrent against the Soviets should have a higher priority than defending our cities against a hypothetical Chinese threat.

Thus, in the early months of 1969, both the Congress and the Administration were reconsidering the Sentinel decision, and many informed (and uninformed) private citizens, including myself, seized the opportunity to make their views known. The Subcommittee on International Organizations and Disarmament (chaired by Senator Albert Gore) of the Senate Foreign Relations Committee and a similar subcommittee of the House (chaired by Representative Clement J. Zablocki) held well-publicized open hearings on the subject.

The new Defense Secretary, former Representative Melvin R. Laird, and the new Deputy Secretary, David Packard, also reviewed the question of whether to deploy Sentinel. They were assisted in this review by John Foster, the Director of Defense Research and Engineering, and Stanley Resor, the Secretary of the Army. Both of these men had served in the same positions under Robert McNamara and Clark Clifford. Similarly involved in this review were two of the abler general officers in the United States Army: Alfred D. Starbird, in charge of the Sentinel program, and Austin R. Betts, the Chief of Army Research and Development. I knew both of these officers well; I had worked closely with Starbird when he was Director of Military Applications for the AEC and I was director of the Livermore Laboratory; I had worked closely with Betts when he was Director of ARPA and I was Director of Defense Research and Engineering.

Also, as usual, new intelligence information was continuing to come in. It was studied and collated by those responsible for doing so, and was fed into the review process.

On March 14, while the Senate hearings were still in progress, President Nixon announced his decision in the matter. He said he had considered three possible courses: going ahead with the Sentinel system as proposed at the end of the Johnson administration, not going ahead with any ABM at all, or going ahead with a modified system. He chose the last of these, and he said that he wanted a system that would protect a part of our Minuteman force in order to increase the credibility of our deterrent, and that he had overruled moving in the direction of a massive city defense because "even starting with a thin system and then going to a heavy system tends to be more provocative in terms of making credible a first-strike capability against the Soviet Union. I want no provocation which might deter arms talks." (At that time, governments on both sides of the Atlantic were looking forward to strategic-arms-limitation talks in the summer of 1969.)

The top civilian defense officials gave this same rationale, although they put a little more emphasis on the "prototype" and "growth-potential" aspects of the system. For simplicity and clarity I shall focus on the Administration's proposal as presented in open session by responsible officials.

This new ABM soon became widely known as the "Safeguard system" for its primary purpose of defending or safeguarding a part of our deterrent forces.

The Senate hearings, which began a little over a week before the President announced his decision, continued into the summer. The majority of those who testified against deployment of an ABM system were persons who had previously held government positions of major responsibility and authority. This group included all of the former Special Assistants to the President for Science and Technology: Killian and Kistiakowsky, who served under Eisenhower; Wiesner, who served under Kennedy; and Hornig, who served under Johnson. It also included Ruina, a former Director of ARPA; Kaysen, an assistant in the White House under Kennedy; George W. Rathjens, a former Chief Scientist of ARPA; and myself. Two other scientists who testified against deployment, Hans Bethe and W. K. H. Panofsky, had been members of the President's Science Advisory Committee—Bethe during the Eisenhower administration and Panofsky during the Kennedy and Johnson administrations. A law professor, Abram Chayes, and two political scientists, Marshall Shulman and Allen Whiting, also testified negatively.

The majority of those who testified for deployment (excluding then current government witnesses) were, curiously, theoretical scientists and mathematicians. This group included William McMillan, Richard Latter, Donald Brennan, Frederick Seitz, Albert Wohlstetter, Freeman Dyson, and Edward Teller. In addition, four former high government officials testified in favor of deployment. Two of these had primarily political backgrounds: Paul Nitze, a former Deputy Secretary of Defense, and Dean Acheson, a former Secretary of State. The other two had primarily technical backgrounds: Charles Herzfeld, another former Director of ARPA, and Daniel Fink, a former Deputy DDRE. One then current member of PSAC, Gordon MacDonald, testified in favor of deployment.

The Senate vote on the ABM came late in July. In order to vote against it, a Senator had to vote for one of two amendments to the Defense Authorization Bill. An amendment offered by Margaret Chase Smith, Republican of Maine, lost on a tie, 50–50; and an amendment by John Sherman Cooper, Republican of Kentucky, lost 49–51.

The Senate opposition to the ABM had been bipartisan. Among Democrats, Fulbright, Gore, Hart, Kennedy, and Symington led the opposition. On the Republican side the leaders were Cooper, Case, and Percy.

The ABM had been widely discussed on other occasions also. On March 4, meetings were held in a number of major academic and research institutions all over the country for the purpose of discussing the proper relationship between such institutions and "war research." Much of these discussions focused on the ABM. At M.I.T. where the idea for the meetings originated, Hans Bethe spoke before a multitude of students and faculty. He started by saying, "You're here because you're against the ABM. I'm here to tell you why you are." The audience was, happily, able to see the joke and laugh at itself. (A few days later, I spoke about the same matter to a large interested group at the Salk Institute in La Jolla.)

Later, as the Senate hearings warmed up, city clubs, local foreign-relations councils, and the like started to sponsor speakers and debates. National as well as local television gave prominent coverage to the subject in their news programs and ran news specials in order to go into greater detail. America had finally become concerned about what the generals and the technologists were doing in her name.

The Administration's spokesmen based their case mainly on the continuing deployment of the very large Soviet ICBM we call the SS-9. They described this ICBM as being able to deliver a twenty-megaton warhead, and they claimed that a Soviet program for developing a MIRV payload capable of delivering three five-megaton warheads was in progress. They further asserted that by the mid-seventies the delivery accuracy of these three individual warheads could be such as to result in a kill probability of ninety-six percent against a Minuteman silo with its current hardness of three hundred pounds per square inch. In effect, this means they were predicting a CEP of about a quarter of a mile. It also means that the Soviets would have to have a capability for replacing each of their missiles that failed during launch, thus completely making up for any residual unreliability in the system. They estimated that 150 SS-9s were then deployed and they projected a growth rate in this figure of about forty per year.

Putting together the projections of numbers and the assumptions about future accuracy, reliability, and ability to replace failed missiles, the Defense Department spokesmen calculated that a preemptive attack in 1975 or 1976 by the Soviet SS-9 force on the U. S. Minuteman force could result in the destruction of all but forty Minutemen. And this number, they asserted, was so small that the ABM system the Soviets could have installed by that time might be able to cope with it. All this long train of estimates, assumptions, and possibilities led Secretary Laird to conclude that the only logical explanation for the SS-9 buildup was that the Soviets were "going for a first-strike capability." The logical response on our part, he argued, was to install an ABM system to defend at least a part of our deterrent so as to deny them such a first-strike capability. One must admit that almost anything is conceivable as far as intentions are concerned, but there certainly are simpler and, it seems to me, more likely explanations.

Probably the simplest of all was apparent in a chart presented before Senator Gore's subcommittee by Deputy Secretary Packard. It showed clearly that until about the beginning of 1967 the Russians had been quite content to be a very poor second in the missile race. Up to that time, we enjoyed a three- or fourfold numerical advantage over them in ICBMs. This is made more puzzling by the fact that all during this period U.S. defense officials found it necessary to boast about how far ahead we were, in order to be able to resist internal pressures for still greater expansion of our offensive forces. It is not unlikely, therefore, that the Russians simply decided to do something dramatic about this large imbalance.

Another possible reason for the deployment of the SS-9, and one that I believe added to the other in the minds of the Russian planners, was that their strategists concluded in the mid-1960s, that, whatever the top officials here might be saying at the time, certain elements would eventually succeed in getting a large-scale ABM system built, and that penetration-aid devices, including multiple warheads, would be needed to meet the challenge. If they did make such a hypothetical prediction, they were, unfortunately, correct. Let us, however, pass on from this question of someone else's intentions and consider whether or not the proposed Safeguard ABM system is a valid, rational, and necessary response to the Russian deployments and developments outlined above.

In order to do so, it will be well to have in mind a picture of the over-all balance in strategic forces. The main components of these forces are presented in a table given below. This table is adapted from Defense Department briefings given during the 1970 ABM debates. The small land-based missiles are Minutemen in the U. S. case and mostly the roughly equivalent S-11s in the Soviet case. The large missiles are Titan IIs in the U. S. case, and the still larger SS-9s in the Soviet case. Not covered are a number of relatively less important "extras" such as the Soviet FOBS (fractional orbital bombardment system), the IRBMs, and the very many U. S. aircraft deployed on carriers, in Europe, and elsewhere.

In the area of defensive systems designed to cope with the offensive systems just outlined, both the U. S. and the U.S.S.R. have defenses against bombers that would be adequate against a prolonged attack using chemical explosives (where ten percent attrition is enough) but certainly inadequate against a nuclear attack (where ten percent penetration is enough). In addition, the U.S.S.R. has an ABM system, much like our old Nike-Zeus system, deployed around Moscow. It appears to

SEPTEMBER 1969 STRATEGIC FORCES

		U.S.	U.S.S.R.
Intercontinental ballistic missiles in hard silos	large	54	about 250
	small	1,000	about 850
Submarine-launched ballistic missiles		656	about 110
Heavy bombers		581	about 140

have virtually no capability against our offensive-missile systems, and it is usually estimated as consisting of less than one hundred antimissile missiles. As we have seen, it was the stimulus, though not the provocation, behind our MIRV development, and thus it has been extremely counterproductive in its goal of defending Moscow.

From a technical point of view and as far as components are concerned, President Nixon's Safeguard system of today is very little different from President Johnson's Sentinel system. There are only minor changes in location of certain components (away from cities), and elements have been added to some of the radars so that they can now observe submarine-launched missiles coming from directions other than directly from the U.S.S.R. and China. As before, the system consists of a long-range interceptor carrying a large nuclear weapon (Spartan), a fast short-range interceptor carrying a nuclear weapon (Sprint), two types of radar (perimeter acquisition radar, or PAR, and missile-site radar, or MSR), a computer for directing the battle, and a command and control system for integrating Safeguard with the national command. I shall not describe the equipment in detail at this point, but shall pass on directly to what I believe can be concluded from the hearings and other public sources about four major questions.

1. Assuming that Safeguard could protect Minuteman, is it needed to protect our deterrent?

Perhaps the clearest explanation of why the answer to this first question is No was given by Wolfgang K. H. Panofsky before the Senate Armed Services Committee in April, 1969. He described how the deterrent consists of three main components: Polaris submarines, bombers, and land-based ICBMs. Each of these components alone is capable of delivering far more warheads than is actually needed for deterrence, and each is currently defended against surprise destruction in a quite different way. ICBMs are in hard silos and are numerous. Polarises are hidden in the seas. Bombers can be placed on various levels of alert and can be dispersed.

Since the warning time in the case of an ICBM attack in the mid-seventies is generally taken as being about thirty minutes, the people who believe that the deterrent may be in serious danger usually imagine that the bombers are attacked by missile submarines and therefore have a warning of only fifteen minutes or less. This is important, because a thirty-minute warning gives the bombers ample time to get off the ground and even fifteen minutes allows about half to get away, according to a report by Clark Clifford when he was Secretary of Defense. In that case, however, an attack on all three components cannot be made simultaneously; that is, if the attacking weapons are launched simultaneously, they cannot arrive simultaneously.

Thus, it is incredible that all three of our deterrent systems could become vulnerable in the same time period, and it is doubly incredible that this could happen without our having sufficient notice to do something about it. There was therefore no basis for a frantic reaction to the hypothetical Russian threat to Minuteman. Still, it was sensible and prudent to begin thinking about the problem, and so we turn to the other questions. We must consider these questions in the technological framework of the mid-1970s, and we shall do this now in the way which defense officials currently seem to favor: by assuming that this is the best of all possible technological worlds, that everything works as intended, and that direct extrapolations of current capabilities are valid.

2. *Assuming that Safeguard works, can it in fact safeguard Minuteman?*

One good approach to this problem is the one used by George W. Rathjens in his testimony before the Senate Armed Services Committee on April 23, 1969. His analysis took as a basis of calculation the implication in Secretary Laird's early testimony that the Minuteman force may become seriously imperiled in the mid-1970s. Rathjens then estimated how many SS-9s would have to be deployed at that time in order to achieve this result. From this number and the estimate of the current number of SS-9s deployed he got a rate of deployment. He also had to make an assumption about how many Sprints and Spartans would be deployed at that time, and his estimates were based on the first phase of Safeguard deployment. These last numbers had not been released, but a range of reasonable values could be guessed from the cost estimate given. Over a fairly wide range of such guesses, Rathjens found that by prolonging the SS-9 production program by a few months the Russians would be able to cope with Safeguard by simply exhausting it and would still have enough warheads left to imperil Minuteman, if that is indeed their intention.

The length of this short safe period does depend on the numbers used in such calculations, and they, of course, can be disputed to a degree. Thus, if one assumes that it takes fewer Russian warheads to imperil Minuteman (it *later* became evident that defense officials were assuming one for one), then the assumed deployment rate is lower and the safe period is lengthened; on the other hand, if one notes that the missile-site radars in our system are one-tenth as hard as even today's silos, then the first attacking warheads, fired directly at the radars, can be smaller and less accurate, so that a higher degree of MIRVing can be used for attacking these radars and a shorter safe period results. To go further, it was suggested that the accuracy–yield combination of the more numerous SS-11s would be sufficient for attacking the missile-site radars, and therefore, if the Russians were to elect such an option, there would be no safe period at all. In short, the most that Safeguard can do is either delay somewhat the date when Minuteman would be imperiled or cause the attacker to build up his forces at a somewhat higher rate if, indeed, imperiling Minuteman by a fixed date is his purpose.

3. Will it work?

By this question I mean: Will operational units be able to intercept enemy warheads accompanied by enemy penetration aids, in an atmosphere of total astonishment and uncertainty? I do not mean: Will test equipment and test crews intercept U. S. warheads accompanied by U. S. penetration aids in a contrived atmosphere? A positive answer to the latter question is a necessary condition for obtaining a positive answer to the former, but it is by no stretch of the imagination a sufficient condition.

This basic question has been attacked from two quite different angles: by examining historical analogies and by examining the technical elements of the problem in detail. Design-oriented people who consider this a purely technical question emphasize the second approach. I believe the question is by no means a purely technical question, and I suggest that the historical-analogy approach is more promising, albeit much more difficult to use correctly.

False analogies are common in this argument. We find that some people say, "You can't tell me that if we can put a man on the moon we can't build an ABM." Others say, "That's what Oppenheimer told us about the hydrogen bomb." These two statements contain the same basic error. They are examples of successes in a contest between technology and nature, whereas the ABM issue involves a contest between two technologies; offensive weapons and penetration aids versus defensive weapons and discrimination techniques. These analogies would be more pertinent if, in the first case, someone were to jerk the moon away just before the astronauts landed, or if, in the second case, nature were to keep changing the nuclear-reaction probabilities all during the development of the hydrogen bomb and once again after it was deployed.

Proper historical analogies should involve modern high-technology defense systems that have actually been installed and used in combat. If one examines the record of such systems, one finds that they do often produce some attrition of the offense, but not nearly enough to be of use against a nuclear attack. The most up-to-date example is provided by the

Russian SAMs and other air defense equipment deployed in North Vietnam. This system worked after a fashion because both the equipment designers and the operating crews had plenty of opportunities to practice against real U. S. targets equipped with real U. S. tactics.

The best example of a U. S. system is somewhat older, but I believe it is still relevant. It is the SAGE system, which I discussed at the beginning of this chapter. To quote from the recent book on the ABM decision prepared by Wiesner, Abram Chayes, and others: "Still, after fifteen years, and the expenditure of more than $20 billion, it is generally conceded that we do not have a significant capability to defend ourselves against a well-planned air attack. The Soviet Union, after even greater effort, has probably not done much better." And in 1970, Secretary Laird said, "The current bomber defense system, as the Congress is well aware, has a limited combat effectiveness and is expensive to operate. . . . We plan to continue the phase-down of the . . . system. . . ."

So much for analogies; let us turn to the Safeguard system itself. Doubts about its being able to work were raised during the public hearings on a variety of grounds, some of which are as follows:

First, and perhaps foremost, there is the remarkable fact that the new Safeguard system and the old Sentinel system use virtually the same hardware, deployed in a very similar manner, and yet they have entirely different primary purposes. Sentinel had as its purpose defending large soft targets against the so-called Chinese threat. The Chinese threat by definition involved virtually no sophisticated penetration aids and no possibilities of exhausting the defense; thus were "solved" two of the most difficult problems that had eliminated Nike-Zeus and Nike-X.

Safeguard has as its primary purpose defending a part of the Minuteman force against a Russian attack. It is not credible that a Russian attack against the part of the Minuteman force so defended would be other than massive and sophisticated, so we are virtually right back to trying to do what in 1967 we said we could not do, and we are trying to do it with no real change in the missiles or the radars. It is true that defending hard points is to a degree easier than defending cities, because interception can be accomplished later and at lower altitudes, thus giving discrimination techniques more time to work. Moreover, only those objects headed for specific small areas must be intercepted. These factors do make the problem easier, but they do not ensure its solution, and plenty of room for doubt remains.

Second, there is the contest between penetration aids and discrimination techniques. This was discussed by Richard Garwin and Hans Bethe in their March, 1968, article in *Scientific American* and was mentioned also in varying degrees of detail by many of those who testified in the spring of 1969 concerning the ABM issue. The Russian physicist Andrei D. Sakharov, in his essay *Thoughts on Progress, Coexistence and Intellectual Freedom,* put the issue this way:

> Improvements in the resistance of warheads to shock waves and the radiation effects of neutron and X-ray exposure, the possibility of mass use of relatively light and inexpensive decoys that are virtually indistinguishable from warheads and exhaust the capabilities of an antimissile defense system, a perfection of tactics of massed and concentrated attacks, in time and space, that overstrain the defense detection centers, the use of orbital and fractional-orbital attacks, the use of active and passive jamming and other methods not disclosed in the press— all of this has created technical and economic obstacles to an effective missile defense that, at the present time, are virtually insurmountable.

I would add only MIRV to Sakharov's list. Pitted against this plethora of penetration aids are various observational methods designed to discriminate the real warheads. Some of the penetration devices obviously work only at high altitudes, but even these make it necessary for the final "sorting" to be delayed, and thus they still contribute to making the defense problem harder. Other devices can continue to confuse the defense even down to low altitudes. Some of the problems the offense presents to the defense can no doubt be solved (and have been solved) when considered separately and in isolation. That is, they can be solved for a time, until the offense designers react. One must have serious reservations, however, whether these problems can ever be solved for any long period in the complex combinations that even a modestly sophisticated attacker can present. Further, such a contest could result in a catastrophic failure of the system in which all or nearly all interceptions fail.

Third, there is the unquantifiable difference between the test range and the real world. The extraordinary efforts of the Air Force to test operationally deployed Minutemen in the late sixties show that it too regards this as an important problem. Moreover, the results of those tests did reveal important weaknesses in the deployed forces. The problem has many aspects: the possible differences between test equipment and deployed equipment; the certain differences between the offensive warheads and penetration aids supplied by us as test targets and the corresponding equipment and tactics the defense must ultimately be prepared to face; the differences between the installation crews at a test site and at a deployment site; the differences in attitudes and motivation between a test crew and an operational crew (even if it is composed of the same men); the differences between men and equipment that have recently been made ready and that everyone is watching and men and equipment that have been standing ready for years during which nothing happened; the differences between the emotional atmosphere where everyone knows it's not "for real" and the emotional atmosphere where no one can believe what he has just been told. It may be that all that enormously complex equipment will be ready to work the very first time it must "for real," and it may be that all those thousands of human beings have performed all their interlocking assignments correctly, but I have very substantial doubts about it.

Fourth, there is the closely related "hair-trigger–stiff-trigger" contradiction. Any active defense system such as Safeguard must sit in readiness for two or four or eight years and then fire at precisely the correct second following a warning time of only minutes. Furthermore, the precision needed for the firing time is so fine that machines must be used to choose the exact instant of firing no matter how the decision to fire is made. In the case of offensive missiles the situation is different in an essential way: Although the maintaining of readiness throughout a long, indefinite period is necessary, the moment of firing is not so precisely controlled in general, and hence human decision-makers, including even those at high levels, may readily be permitted to play a part in the decision-making process. Thus if we wish to be certain that the defense will respond under conditions of surprise, the trigger of the ABM system, unlike the triggers of the ICBMs and Polarises, must be continuously sensitive and ready—in short, a hair trigger—for indefinitely long periods of time. (This distinction applies only to the past and present. In the future, some offensive systems will also require "hair triggers.")

On the other hand, it is obvious that we cannot afford to have an ABM missile fire by mistake or in response to a false alarm. Indeed, in 1968 the Army went to some pains to assure residents of areas near proposed Sentinel sites that it was imposing requirements to ensure against the accidental launching of the missile and the subsequent detonation of the nuclear warhead it carries. Moreover, Army officials assured the public that no ABM missiles would ever be launched without the specific approval of "the highest authorities."

These two requirements—a hair trigger so that the system

can cope with a surprise attack, and a stiff trigger so that it will never go off accidentally or without proper authorization —are, I believe, contradictory ones. If the system cannot be fired without approval of "the highest authorities," then the probability of its being fired under conditions of surprise is less than it would be otherwise. This probability depends to a degree on the highly classified technical details of the command and control system, but in the last analysis it depends more on the fact that "the highest authority" is a human being and therefore subject to all the failures and foibles pertaining thereto.

This brings us to the principal question: *Anyway, what harm can it do?*

We have just found that the total deterrent is very probably not in peril, that the Safeguard system as described by the Nixon Administration cannot safeguard Minuteman even if it "works," that there is, to say the least, considerable uncertainty whether or not it will "work." Nonetheless, if there were no harm in it, we might be prudent and follow the basic motto of the arms race: "Let us err on the side of military safety." There seem to be many answers to the question of what harm it would do to build an ABM system. First of all, such a system would cost large sums of money needed for nondefense purposes. Second, it would divert money and attention from what may be better military solutions to the strategic problems posed by the Administration. Third, it would intensify the arms race. All these considerations were discussed at the 1969 hearings: I shall comment here only on the third, the arms-race implications of the ABM decision.

It is often said that an ABM system is not an accelerating element in the arms race, because it is intrinsically defensive. For example, during the 1969 hearings Senator Henry M. Jackson of Washington, surely one of the best-informed Senators in this field, said essentially that, and he quoted Premier Kosygin as having said the same thing. I believe such a notion is in error and is based on what we may call "the fallacy of the last move."

I believe that in the real world of constant change in both the technology and the deployed numbers of all kinds of strategic-weapons systems, ABM systems are accelerating elements in the arms race. At the beginning of this decade we began to hear about a possible Russian ABM system, and we became concerned about its potential effects on our ICBM and Polaris systems. In response the MIRV concept was invented. Today there are additional justifications for MIRV besides penetration, but that is how it started. Now the possibility of a Russian MIRV is used as one of the main arguments in support of the Safeguard system. Thus, we have come one full turn around the arms-race spiral. No one in 1960 and 1961 thought through the potential destabilizing effects of multiple warheads, and certainly no one predicted or even could have predicted that the inexorable logic of the arms race would carry us directly from Russian talk in 1960 about defending Moscow against missiles to a requirement for hardpoint defense of offensive-missile sites in the U. S. in 1969.

By the same token I am sure the Russians did not foresee the large increase in deployed U. S. warheads that will ultimately result from their ABM-missile deployment and that made it so counterproductive. Similarly, no one today can describe in detail the chain reaction the Safeguard deployment would lead to, but it is easy to see the seeds of a future acceleration of the arms race in the Safeguard deployment. Russian offense planners are going to look at it and say something such as: "It may not work, but we must be prudent and assume it will." They may then plan further deployments or more complex penetration systems, or maybe they will go to more dangerous systems such as bombs in orbit. A little later, when some of our optimistic statements about how it will do the job it is supposed to do have become part of history, our strategic planners are going to look at Safeguard and say something such as: "Maybe it will work as they said, but we must be prudent and assume it will not, and, besides, now look at what the Russians are doing."

This approach to strategic thinking, known in the trade as "worst-case analysis," leads to a completely hopeless situation in which there is no possibility of achieving a state of affairs that both sides would consider as constituting parity. Moreover, our defense establishment, and presumably theirs too, will not even consider arms-control measures except, as an absolute minimum, under conditions that it considers to constitute parity. Thus, there is no possibility of stopping the arms race except by political action *outside* the two defense establishments.

I also mentioned in my own testimony at the ABM hearings that "we may further expect deployment of these ABM systems to lead to the persistent query 'But how do you know it *really* works?' and thus to increase the pressures against the current limited nuclear-test ban as well as to work against amplifying it." I mentioned this then, and I mention it again now, in the hope that it will become a self-defeating prediction.

11
OTHER LESSONS
FROM THE ABM DEBATE

What are the basic forces behind ABM deployment and what do they really demand? A partial answer to this question may be found in the testimony of Donald Hornig, Lyndon Johnson's Special Assistant for Science and Technology and, in accord with custom, also Chairman of the President's Science Advisory Committee (PSAC). Hornig served in these capacities for five years, from January, 1964, through December, 1968, and before that he was one of the members of PSAC. He therefore had had the opportunity to watch the parade of the various versions of ABM from a grandstand seat for as long a time as anyone. Like all the other former Special Assistants to the President for Science and Technology, he opposed the deployment of the Safeguard system. He said:

> If I were convinced that the protection of a credible deterrent were indeed the eventual goal and that Safeguard was the best way to protect that deterrent, I would support it. But the uneasy feeling persists that although Presidents may change, Secretaries of Defense may come and go, the philosophies enunciated by political leaders may change, the design of our ABM system hardly changes at all. It includes

the same radars, the same rockets, and largely the same deployment which was contemplated for the "heavy" defense. Safeguard continues to look like a first step toward a much bigger, more expensive and still ineffective system.

To many of the rest of us, too, the ABM appeared to have all the characteristics of a solution in search of a problem. As I have already remarked, this characteristic shows up all too often in our defense research and development programs, especially in the field of nuclear weaponry. I suggest the fundamental reason the ABM decision came up in 1969 was that ten years earlier Secretary of Defense McElroy, in dividing up the space and missile roles and missions among the three services, assigned the ABM to the Army as its only large sophisticated missile program. This decision created a situation in which for many years the lives and careers of many able persons have been closely entwined with the life and fate of one single program: the Army's ABM. This includes not only the civilians employed in the program office and by the main contractors, it also includes uniformed personnel and, probably just as importantly, a whole host of part-time advisers at all levels. If, in fact, we examine closely the testimony given by persons who are part-time advisers to the defense establishment and who were also in favor of the deployment of the present ABM system, we find that with only very few exceptions they favor Safeguard not as an end in itself, not for the purposes which the President laid down, but rather as a prototype of something else much bigger and much more complex and enormously more expensive. They want a grand system which they hope could protect not only the deterrent but also the rest of what goes to make up the United States of America. In short, they want to do a job which almost certainly cannot be done even if, by some magic, it could be done as the "last move" in the arms race. Equally certainly, it would result in a reaction by the Soviets which would more than offset even the theoretical capability of such a system, and, again equally certainly, it would cost vastly more money than the sums anyone is now talking about. Looking at the problem this way, we can see why it is that as a practical matter it is almost impossible for the United States to build a "thin" ABM system.

Let us turn now to a somewhat more general question: Can any ABM system be made to work? If one of the main weaknesses in Safeguard is that it is too thin and hence easily defeated by simple exhaustion, how about a thicker system? The answer to such questions has to depend in part on what "work" means, and that definition is not always as simple as it might seem. In fact, the question "Will it work?" has three quite distinct meanings.

First, as discussed earlier, it may mean, Will it work on the test range? That is, will it regularly and reliably intercept the best mockups we know how to make of enemy warheads accompanied by enemy penetration aids and tactics? A favorable answer to this question is a necessary though not a sufficient condition for having any confidence in the system in question. And studying this question is an essential part of the design and development of any system. Experimentally verifying a favorable answer to this question would normally precede a decision to deploy, though under certain emergency conditions a high promise that such will be obtained might temporarily suffice. An ABM system that will work in this sense may well be possible.

Second, we may mean, Will it really work when the "balloon goes up"? That is, if a real enemy fires a real enemy warhead accompanied by real enemy penetration aids at a time of his choosing in an atmosphere of incredulity, will an operational unit manned by regular troops intercept it? Here we are dealing again with the difference between the test range and the real world. It is, of course, always impossible to be absolutely certain of the answer to this type of "Will it work?" question until after the war is over, so for all new military systems we have to rely on theoretical predictions in dealing with it. However, such predictions are much more difficult to make about missile-defense systems than about offensive systems. The reason for this is to be found in certain intrinsic differences between offensive and defensive missiles. Once an offensive warhead is finally on its way, it need not "do" anything until it contacts the ground or arrives at some predetermined height, at which time it has only to explode. A defensive system must, in a matter literally of only some seconds, puzzle its way through the deceptive devices and tactics of the total offensive payload and then explode its warhead at precisely the correct time and place, neither of which can be predetermined before the battle starts. This latter is intrinsically a more complex problem, and hence the subtle differences between the test range and the real world matter much more in the case of defensive missiles than in the case of offensive missiles. I have never heard of an ABM proposal which would lead me to have much confidence in a positive answer to this second type of "Will it work?" question.

The third meaning of the "Will it work?" question is largely political rather than technological in nature, and, as a result, it is by far the most important. A general way of phrasing this question is, Will it help its possessor to achieve some particular political objective? More specific ways of phrasing this third question might be, Will it contribute to deterring war? or even Will it make a preemptive attack more promising? The answers to these questions, unlike the answers to the first two, do not depend directly on what the technological facts *really* are, but rather on what the political and military (not the scientific) leadership on each side *thinks* they may be. Presumably, someone planning a preemptive attack would make a most serious attempt to estimate conservatively just how much damage the retaliation that such an attack inevitably provoked would wreak on his own country. Clearly, a thick ABM system without serious soft spots such as Safeguard has could be just enough to make the difference in a go–no-go judgment by the decision-makers.

For example, if only the side considering making a surprise attack had such a system, and the system defended that side's population, it would make such an attack more promising. On the other hand, if only the side to be attacked had such a system, and if the system defended that side's retaliatory forces, then it would make a surprise attack look less promising. However, if each side possessed such a system, then these things would tend to balance each other off, and we would, as usual, be back more or less where we started, with neither of us having achieved any net gain.

During the 1969 ABM debates, several ways for making a more effective system were discussed. These usually involved both making the system thicker (i.e., composed of much larger amounts of all kinds of equipment) and removing the most serious soft spots. Some suggested that this last be done by duplicating or triplicating the large missile-site radars. Others suggested that the radar part of the system be completely redesigned with the objective of replacing the current large single radar with a large number of small cheap radars. I believe that a combination of such ideas could lead to a system that would be effective in the political or strategic sense. However, I also believe such a system would be very expensive, certainly costing more than fifty billion dollars, and it would make the difference only in the extremely unlikely circumstance that everything else looked favorable to a preemptive attack.

Thus, under certain fortunately very unlikely circumstances, possession of an ABM system could produce just enough false confidence to make a holocaust more likely. This is not something dreamed up late at night after a meal of pickles and apple pie: I have heard a number of high American general officers and civilian officials, including Nelson Rockefeller, make remarks to the effect that defenses (including shelters) were needed in order to "stiffen the backbone of the American people." In other words, many people want such defenses because they want the possibility of nuclear war to be less unthinkable and hence less of a deterrent to other types of foreign political adventures. I am pleased to be able to report that I never heard a United States Secretary of Defense make such a remark, even though I was, for a number of years, often present in discussions of the type that would have provoked such a remark if it had been an expression of real belief.

Other interesting side issues came up during the ABM debates. One of the most important had to do with the proper role of the expert in making decisions of the kind then under discussion. Practically all of the nongovernment witnesses heard by the two principal Senate committees were experts at something relevant to the discussions—usually, but not always, technology. These experts frequently disagreed flatly with each other. To some people, these disagreements among experts were something new. They expressed dismay, and plaintively asked if the experts cannot agree among themselves, how is a poor layman to decide?

Looking more deeply into the matter, we find that the experts not only disagreed on the answers, they also disagreed over what the important issues were. Further, the disagreements were not over technical facts, but rather over judgments and predictions: What *will* the Soviet technological response to our ABM or MIRV be? *Will* it "work" against a real attack seven or ten years from now? How *will* their (or our) assessment of that question influence their (or our) decision-makers? How *will* spending so much money this way affect other elements of our military power? How *will* it affect the domestic scene? These are all basically nontechnological questions. To be sure, technological facts, to a degree, are relevant to all of them, in some cases very much so. But they do not have numerical answers and they generally transcend the kind of questions that do.

Much of the confusion and dispute that have arisen over this matter of the role of the expert derives from a failure to recognize the very fundamental difference between the kind of expertise and knowledge needed to design a weapons system and the entirely different kind of knowledge and wisdom needed to judge one. To take an easier case, consider the lunar landing. If you want to know how to get to the moon, ask a rocket expert; if you want to know who should pilot the spacecraft, ask experts in space medicine and psychology; if you want to know what ought to be done after getting there, ask a geophysicist. But if you want to know whether someone should go there in the first place, ask any sensitive informed person. A politically literate housewife has at least as much business answering that last question as any of the experts mentioned, unless, perhaps, her husband makes his living in the space program.

The same reasoning applies to the ABM argument. If you want to know what a Soviet warhead looks like, ask the intelligence experts; if you want to know what radar wavelength to use to detect that warhead behind a cloud of ionized air produced by a previous nuclear burst, ask a physicist; if you want to know what the options are regarding the nuclear explosives to be used in its interception, ask the nuclear-weapons designers. If you want to know how a Soviet operations analyst would react to a given move, ask a U. S. operations analyst. But if you want to know whether or not to deploy Safeguard, there is no better place to go to than the usual political arena. Compared, for example, to the question of what to do about urban problems and racism, the question of what to do about the Safeguard ABM is certainly simpler and more straightforward and probably less important.

The same thing, of course, applies much more broadly: all

major weapons systems and defense policies should receive the kind of political and public scrutiny that the ABM received in 1969 and 1970. We must hope that the precedents established in those hearings will be used in other similar cases.

The man who claims, in a political argument, to have special understanding of some abstruse or arcane theory involved in weapons design and the man who claims to know a secret you don't know may indeed be privy to certain facts not generally available, but nearly always they are using such claims as a means to avoid arguing about the issues that really count. Such persons may not be doing so deliberately; most often, I think, they are themselves deceived and they simply do not understand the difference between designing something and judging something. They get caught up in an argument that says, "If it's feasible it must be useful; if it's useful and involves defense it must be essential; and since only I really understand how it works, my judgment is paramount." It is easy to be deceived by details and secrets. A man who spends a long time and a great deal of his personal psychic energy on solving a particular specialized problem can very easily believe that he has solved more than just that problem when he finally does succeed; and the man who knows a long list of secret details, every one of which may be iffy and uncertain, can easily lose sight of the bigger issues in which they are imbedded. As the political columnist Joseph Kraft said in discussing the Vietnam War, "Whom the gods would destroy in Vietnam, they first fill full of detailed information."

The arguments over the kind and degree of expertise needed in such matters was epitomized for me during the ABM hearings in the remarks of two quite different men: Donald Brennan, a mathematician and one-time president and still a member of the Hudson Institute (the "think tank" founded by Herman Kahn), and Senator Henry M. Jackson, a very able lawyer with long experience in defense matters. It happened that they both held that Safeguard should be deployed, but the remarks I have in mind (which they did not make to each other or in reference to each other) bear sharply on this question of the "expert" role from opposite points of view.

Brennan, in a discussion of whether it was appropriate for the Senate to decide whether Safeguard should be deployed, said:

It is possible to conceive that the detailed scale and timing of expenditures for protecting offensive forces could properly come under Congressional scrutiny, though this would represent a new thing and I am not sure I should favor it. It would, in any event, have to be done in executive sessions, with sensitive information. It does not seem at all feasible to me to have such scrutiny of the decision as to the best means of providing the protection. The judgment about the best means should be based on a complex of factors that can scarcely be grasped whole by a full-time Secretary of Defense. That a committee of the Congress could meaningfully penetrate such a judgment seems to me most unlikely.

Subsequent testimony and later debates made it clear that Brennan had no doubts about his own ability to scrutinize such decisions. But in the course of the same hearings, and at the end of an unusually long day of testimony, Senator Jackson expressed the opposite point of view, as the following excerpts from the transcript of these hearings show.

SENATOR JACKSON: Mr. Chairman, I should just like to make a brief observation. In the fall of 1949 —I was a Member of the House at the time—I was appointed by the late Senator Brien McMahon to the so-called Hydrogen Bomb Subcommittee. It was our task to make a recommendation whether this

country ought to go ahead with the development of
the hydrogen bomb. . . .

Senator Jackson then described how the subcommittee decided, against the advice of most experts, to go ahead with
the H-bomb, and he continued:

> I mention all of this, Mr. Chairman, to emphasize
> that we have to weigh the arguments . . . that we
> have to look at all points of view—and in the end
> use our judgment. *I do not think we laymen need be
> embarrassed in trying to weigh scientific judgments.**
> My own experience, which goes back a number of
> years in the House and Senate, has never left me
> with an inferiority complex in trying to deal with
> these problems that involve great scientific exper-
> tise . . . in 1949 every member of the blue-ribbon
> Science Advisory Committee of the Atomic Energy
> Commission, except Dr. Glenn Seaborg, who was
> not present, was opposed to going ahead with the
> hydrogen bomb, for the various reasons that have
> been alluded to here. That Advisory Committee was
> a Who's Who of science.

The brilliant physicist and weapons expert W. K. H. Panofsky, who was a witness at the hearings, responded at this point:

> I just wanted to add I agree very much with Sen-
> ator Jackson's remarks that decisions have to be
> made by the nonprofessionals, but they should be
> taken with the best information the professionals can
> provide. Also I am sure, as you have found out to-
> day, that the testimony which professional witnesses

---

* My italics.

can give is limited because the future is involved and thus judgment and knowledge are both involved.

When I discussed the nuclear airplane (ANP) I mentioned a quite different kind of intervention by politicians in a technical program. Then the politicians persisted in concerning themselves with *how* to go about developing the power plant for a nuclear aircraft. In particular, they tried to insist on a particular sequence of developmental steps (all of which would be, to be sure, ultimately necessary). The result was a mess, and the nuclear airplane was never built. The present situation is very different. The Senate did not try to determine *how* an ABM system should be built; rather, the debate concerned *whether* it should be built. As I've already said, in my view there is no superior forum for a discussion of this kind of question.

What about shelters, another device often proposed for making nuclear war less "unthinkable?" Shelters are usually spoken of as being "passive defenses," in contrast to ABM systems, which constitute one kind of "active" defense.

Passive defenses suffer from the same fundamental failings as active defenses. Those which are inexpensive enough and unobtrusive enough to be acceptable will neither contribute to the credibility of our deterrent nor substantially reduce casualties if nuclear war occurs. Those which could reduce casualties (and conceivably contribute to the deterrent by so doing) are so extremely expensive and would so disrupt and change our whole way of life that they are completely unacceptable to most persons who have considered them seriously, including me.

In any speculation about the kind of attack to which this country might be exposed, it is useful to note where the military targets are located. Many of the missile bases are, in fact, far from the largest cities. Other key military installations, however, are not so located. Boston, New York, Philadelphia, Seattle, San Francisco, Los Angeles (Long Beach), and San Diego all have important naval bases. Essential command and control centers are located in and near Denver, Omaha, and Washington, D. C. The roll call could be extended to include other major cities containing military installations that would have to be attacked in any major assault on this country. The list does not stop with these; it is only prudent to suppose still other cities would come under attack, because there is no way to know in advance what the strategy may be.

The only kind of shelter that has been seriously considered for other than certain key military installations is the fallout shelter. By definition, fallout shelters offer protection against nothing but fallout and provide virtually no protection against blast, fire storms and other direct effects such as would occur in all the cities named above and others like them. Some people have tried to calculate the percentage of the population that would be saved by fallout shelters in the event of a massive attack, but since the form is unknowable the calculations are nonsensical. Even for the people who really would be protected by fallout shelters the big problem is not a problem in the physical theory of gamma-ray attenuation, which can be neatly computed, but rather the sociological problem of the sudden initiation of general chaos, which is not subject to numerical analysis.

So far, for these and other reasons, the government and the people of the U. S. have always rejected proposals for major fallout-shelter programs. But suppose, in spite of all this, the country were to take fallout shelters seriously and build them in every city and town. The people living in metropolitan areas that qualify as targets because they contain essential military installations and the people living in metropolitan areas that might be targeted as a matter of deliberate policy would soon recognize that relatively lightly constructed fallout shelters could not be adequate to protect them from direct blast effects. Then the same logic that led to the construction of fallout shelters in the first place would lead inevitably to the more heavily constructed, much more expensive blast shelter.

After large numbers of blast shelters were built and evenly distributed throughout the metropolitan community, people would soon realize that shelters alone are not enough. Accidental alarms, even in tautly disciplined military installations, have shown that people do not always take early warnings seriously. Even if they did, a fifteen- to thirty-minute "early" warning provides less than enough time to seal the population into shelters. Accordingly, the logical next step is the live-in and work-in blast shelter, leading to still further disruption and distortion of civilization. There is no logical termination of the line of reasoning that starts with belief in the usefulness of fallout shelters; the logic of this attempt to solve the problem of national security leads to a diverging series of ever more grotesque measures. This is to say, in so many words, that if the arms race continues its current tempo and if we turn seriously to civil defense as a "solution," 1984 is more than just a date on the calendar fourteen years hence.

The preceding four chapters of this book have dealt with the deployment and development of strategic weapons in the period 1961–70. They could be summarized as follows:

1. During the first half of the sixties, the U. S. research and development program relating to strategic-weapons systems was largely one of continuation and consolidation of the programs initiated in the fifties. Thus, the program in this area was characterized by fewer false starts and less unnecessary duplication than formerly. (In some other areas, such as development related to tactical warfare, the opposite may have been true, but that is outside the scope of this book.)

2. The most important of the few new development programs that were initiated during the sixties was MIRV. It threatened to have a very destabilizing effect on the arms race, more so than was at first realized.

3. ABM development continued throughout the sixties. As

in the fifties, proposals to deploy an ABM system continued to be rejected, until late in 1967. At that time it was claimed that the possibility of a Chinese missile threat seemed to "marginally" justify a thin deployment, and this was authorized without much argument. In 1969, after a long public debate, deployment of a different system, the Safeguard ABM, was only narrowly authorized by the Senate. The principal objective of the Safeguard program was said to be protecting the deterrent and maintaining its credibility. Such additional protection is not now needed, and if it were, Safeguard would not provide it. Its deployment may well turn out to be the most costly and most futile of all our excesses in strategic arms deployment.

4. ABM and MIRV both epitomize the accelerating trend toward complexity and a concomitant need for a more highly automated, quicker response. The main dangers in this trend are three: it may result in placing too high a premium on going first; it probably increases the danger of accidental war; and it surely accelerates the trend in the seemingly inexorable transfer of authority over certain life-and-death decisions from statesmen and politicians to soldiers and technicians, from high levels to low levels, and from human beings to machines.

5. The growth of the stockpiles of nuclear weapons in terms of their total explosive yield pretty much stopped in the United States in the mid-sixties. It may still be continuing in the U.S.S.R., which has remained somewhat behind in this area.

6. The deployments of the various types of strategic missiles in terms of numbers were all finally determined in the United States in the early sixties. In the merciless glare of hindsight, I think they were all quite excessive; at least, they ran far ahead of the corresponding deployments in the Soviet Union. Soviet deployments of ICBMs did not catch up with ours until the very end of the sixties; Soviet deployments of submarine-launched missiles similar to our Polaris or Poseidon are still far behind ours in 1970, but could catch up in a few more

years if present building rates continue. Soviet intercontinental-bomber deployments are still lagging and show no sign of catching up. In more qualitative terms, the total explosive power deliverable by Soviet missiles is greater than the corresponding United States total, but U. S. bomber capabilities more than make up for this difference, and U. S. MIRV multiplicities are much larger than anything yet shown by the U.S.S.R.

12

THE ULTIMATE ABSURDITY

The actions and processes described in this book have led to two absurd situations.

The first of these absurdities has been with us for some time, and has come to be widely recognized for what it is. It lies in the fact that ever since World War II the military power of the United States has been steadily increasing, while at the same time our national security has been rapidly and inexorably decreasing. The same thing is happening to the Soviet Union.

The second of these absurdities is still in an early stage and, for reasons of secrecy, is not yet so widely recognized as the first. It lies in the fact that in the United States the power to decide whether or not doomsday has arrived is in the process of passing from statesmen and politicians to lower-level officers and technicians and, eventually, to machines. Presumably, the same thing is happening in the Soviet Union.

At the end of World War II, the United States was, as it had been for more than a century, invulnerable to a direct attack by a foreign power. Just a few years later, the development of the atomic bomb by the Soviet Union ended that ideal state of affairs, perhaps forever.

By the early 1950s the U.S.S.R., on the basis of its own unilateral decision to accept the inevitable retaliation, could have launched an attack against the U. S. with bombers carrying fission bombs. Most of these bombers would have penetrated our defenses and the American casualties could have numbered in the tens of millions.

By the mid-sixties, the U.S.S.R., again on the basis of its own decision to accept the inevitable retaliation, could have launched an attack on the U. S. using intercontinental missiles and bombers carrying thermonuclear weapons. This time the number of American casualties could very well have been on the order of 100 million.

This steady decrease in national security did not result from any inaction on the part of responsible U. S. military and civilian authorities. It resulted from the systematic exploitation of the products of modern science and technology by the U.S.S.R. The air defenses deployed by the U. S. during the 1950s and 1960s might have reduced somewhat the number of casualties that the country might have otherwise sustained, but their existence did not substantially modify this picture. Nor could it have been altered by any other defense measures that might have been taken but that for one reason or another were not.

From the Soviet point of view the picture is similar but much worse. The military power of the U.S.S.R. has been steadily increasing since it became an atomic power in 1949. Soviet national security, however, has been steadily decreasing. Hypothetically the U. S. could unilaterally decide to destroy the U.S.S.R., and the U.S.S.R. would be absolutely powerless to prevent it. That country could only, at best, seek to wreak revenge through the retaliatory capability it would then have left.

Each of us has lived as the pawn of the other's whim—or calculation—for the past twenty years.

The first absurdity is the simple, direct, and probably inevitable result of the interaction of modern science and technology with the chronic military confrontation between the two superpowers. The nuclear-arms race, then, is simply an especially dangerous manifestation of a deeper struggle. This deeper struggle in turn owes its existence to historical forces and tensions that I have not attempted to discuss here. Seemingly, statesmen so far have not been able to cope successfully with this underlying struggle.

Only concerted action by the two superpowers can completely do away with this first absurdity. The long series of closely interrelated actions and reactions by each of them has led to a situation of such complexity that only a similar series of interdigitated arms control and disarmament steps can undo it.

But even if the basic causes of the arms race have been and remain beyond the reach of American statesmen and politicians, its rate and scale have been largely subject to our control. Over the last thirty years we have repeatedly taken unilateral actions that have unnecessarily accelerated the race. These actions have led to the accumulation of unnecessarily large numbers of oversized weapons. In short, these actions have led to the present situation of gross overkill. I do not mean to imply by anything I have written that the Soviets are blameless for accelerating the arms race. The Russian penchant for secrecy, the closed nature of Soviet society, and, for a time, Stalin's visible paranoia—all these are parts of the reciprocating engine that drives the arms race.

I have emphasized American actions partly because I shared responsibility for some of them, partly because I know the details involved in most of the rest and hence understand them far better than I do Russian actions, but most importantly because of a fact that many people sense but do not quite grasp: In the large majority of cases the initiative has been in our hands.

Our unilateral decisions have set the rate and scale for most of the individual steps in the strategic-arms race. In many cases we started development before they did and we easily established a large and long-lasting lead in terms of deployed numbers and types. Examples include the A-bomb itself, intercontinental bombers, submarine-launched ballistic missiles, and MIRV. In other instances, the first development steps were taken by the two sides at about the same time, but immediately afterward our program ran well ahead of theirs both in the development of further types and applications and in the deployment of large numbers. Such cases include the mighty H-bomb and, very probably, military space applications. In some cases, to be sure, they started development work ahead of us and arrived first at the stage where they were able to commence deployment. But we usually reacted so strongly that our deployments and capabilities soon ran far ahead of theirs and we, in effect, even here, determined the final size of the operation. Such cases include the intercontinental ballistic missile and, though it is not strictly a military matter, manned space flight. There are, of course, a few instances where each side has taken actions not yet duplicated by the other. Only the Soviets have deployed the fractional orbital bombardment system, albeit in very small numbers. Only we have had an extensive system of overseas bomber bases surrounding the other side's homeland and a fleet of widely deployed aircraft carriers having a very powerful strategic bombardment capability even if that is not their only purpose or even their major purpose. (I have excluded from consideration all weapons systems, such as Soviet IRBMs and our tactical fighter-bombers, which cannot be readily used against the homelands of the two superpowers.)

The second absurdity—the steady transfer of life-and-death authority from the high levels to low levels, and from human beings to machines—stems from two root causes. One of these is the development and deployment of weapons systems designed in such a way as to require complex decisions to be made in extremely short times. The other is the sheer size and wide dispersal of our nuclear-weapons arsenal.

As we have seen, deployment of MIRV by both sides, coupled with advances in accuracy and reliability, will put a very high premium on the use of the frightful launch-on-warning tactic and may place an even higher premium on a preemptive strike strategy. Under such circumstances, any fixed land-based-missile system must be able to launch its missiles so soon after receipt of warning that high-level human authorities cannot be included in a decision-making process without seriously degrading the system, unless perhaps such authorities have been properly preprogrammed to produce the "right" decision in the short time that might be available to them. And an identical situation applies to any ABM system. After years of waiting, but only minutes of warning, it must respond at the precisely correct second. In order to have any chance of being effective, it must have a "hair trigger." Thus, we seem to be heading for a state of affairs in which the determination of whether or not doomsday has arrived will be made either by an automatic device designed for the purpose or by a pre-programmed President who, whether he knows it or not, will be carrying out orders written years before by some operations analyst.

Such a situation must be called the ultimate absurdity. It would involve making the ultimate decision in an absurd manner, and it would almost surely be more dangerous and insidious than the situation that would result from the invention and deployment of what others have called the ultimate weapon.

The sheer size of the huge nuclear-weapons arsenal and its very great dispersal is leading us in the same direction. The proper command and control of these weapons requires a correspondingly large and complex system reaching down from the President, whose authorization to use nuclear weapons is required by law, to the many soldiers and technicians at lower levels who actually have physical custody of the weapons and the buttons that fire them. All kinds of complicated technical and organizational schemes have been invented and introduced to inhibit any unauthorized use of a nuclear weapon. These include the so-called "permissive-action link" (PAL), the "two-key" type of control system, and the "fail-safe" technique employed by our SAC bombers. So far, these have worked, but no one can be certain they will continue to do so indefinitely. Some of these controls, schemes, and devices are cumbersome and awkward. They "get in the way" and they reduce the state of readiness of the various elements of the stockpile. A number of the schemes have been unpopular with the military services from the beginning, and the introduction of some of them has been resisted.

Some people would like to eliminate the distinction between ordinary and nuclear weapons that now exist in most people's minds. If they succeed, even in part, can we expect these extraordinary control measures to continue in force?

Can we rely on the Soviets to invent and institute the same kind of controls? What will happen as advances in our weapons technology require them to put more and more emphasis on the readiness and the quick responsiveness of their weapons? Do they have the necessary level of sophistication to solve the contradiction inherent in the need for a "hair trigger" (so that their systems will respond in time) and a "stiff trigger" (so that they won't fire accidentally)? How good are their computers at recognizing false alarms? How good is the command and control system for the Polaris-type submarine fleet now being rapidly, if belatedly, deployed by the Soviets? Is it fail-safe?

It cannot be emphasized too strongly that unfavorable answers to these questions about *their* capability mean diminished national security for *us*. Yet there is no way for us to assure favorable answers to them. The only way we can reestablish something like our former level of national security and safety is by eliminating the need to ask them. Strategic weapons must be designed so that no premium is put on a preemptive attack and so that there is no need for the kind of "hair trigger" epitomized in the launch-on-warning concept. Their numbers must not be so great and their dispersal not so wide that such long and complex chains of command are necessary. Weapons systems that do not fit these characteristics must be eliminated. The distinction between ordinary weapons and nuclear weapons must be reinforced and not weakened.

What underlies these overreactions and technological excesses? The answer is very largely patriotic zeal, exaggerated prudence, and a sort of religious faith in technology. Malice, greed, and lust for power are not the main sources of our trouble. In a way, that's too bad; if evil men were the progenitors of these dangerous errors we could expose them and root them out and all would be well. But dealing with errors committed by sincere men acting in good faith is extremely difficult, if not impossible. And the guilty men and organizations are to be found at all levels of government and in all segments of society: Presidents, Presidential candidates; governors and mayors, members of Congress, civilian officials and military officers; business executives and labor leaders; famous scientists and run-of-the-mill engineers; writers and editorialists; and just plain folks.

The various individual promoters of the arms race are stimulated sometimes by patriotic zeal, sometimes by a desire to go along with the gang, sometimes by crass opportunism, and sometimes by simple fear of the unknown. They are inspired by ingenious and clever ideas, challenged by bold statements of real and imaginary military requirements, stimulated to match or exceed technological progress by the other side or even by a rival military service here at home, and victimized by rumors and phony intelligence. Some have been lured by the siren call of rapid advancement, personal recognition, and unlimited opportunity, and some have been bought by promises of capital gains. Some have sought out and even made up problems to fit the solution they have spent much of their lives discovering and developing. A few have used the arms race to achieve other, often hidden objectives.

Nearly all such individuals have had a deep long-term involvement in the arms race. They derive either their incomes, their profits, or their consultant fees from it. But much more important than money as a motivating force are the individuals' own psychic and spiritual needs; the majority of the key individual promoters of the arms race derive a very large part of their self-esteem from their participation in what they believe to be an essential—even a holy—cause.

The organizations these men belong to or represent run the gamut from the Pentagon to the National Defense Industries Association, from the Navy League to the local Rotary, from university departments to the PTA. The strongest and most aggressive of them derive their very *raison d'être* from the arms race. When the principal programs or activities of such organizations are threatened, they react as if endowed with the instincts of living beings. In this book I have expanded on examples of this phenomenon in the reactions of the General Electric Propulsion Division and the Joint Committee on Atomic Energy whenever reductions in the nuclear-airplane program loomed, in the reactions of not only national but also local politicians to attempts to make sense out of the B-70 program, and in the reactions of the Army missile-development organization when it was becoming clear that its beloved Jupiter was no more than a backup to a stopgap. These three cases are, it must be emphasized, only examples; similar events differing only in nonessential details made it very difficult to cancel the Skybolt, the Dyna-Soar, the Manned Orbiting Laboratory, the Navaho, the Snark, and many, many others.

At various times, pride and arguments over pecking order, rather than threats of cancellation, have provided a major stimulus to the arms race. When outer space exploded on the political scene and replaced atomic energy as the sexiest technological area in which the Congress was directly involved, the various Armed Services Committees and subcommittees and the Joint Committee for Atomic Energy jockeyed for legislative control over it. In the process, they stimulated and promoted a number of expensive technological developments that were either unnecessary (large-scale nuclear auxiliary power) or premature (nuclear rocket propulsion) or nonsensical (controlled thermonuclear rockets).

The intense interservice rivalry over roles and missions in space and long-range missilery did the same thing, only more so. Many programs had as one of their main (but hidden) objectives the preemption or recapture of some particular position in the roles-and-missions struggle. Skybolt, Thor, Wizard and the early communications-relay satellites are some of the more obvious instances.

Occasionally wider and more complex power struggles result in programs being continued long after all logic said they should be halted. Such cases include the struggle over the nuclear airplane—a convoluted and long-drawn-out contest among the JCAE, the AEC, the Air Force, the Navy and the Office of the Secretary of Defense—as well as the B-70 battle fought by the Secretary of Defense, the Air Staff, the aerospace industry and the House Armed Services Committee.

Partly as a result of participation in this series of long-drawn-out and sometimes bitter struggles, and partly just due to long association, strong personal bonds and a spirit of camaraderie have built up among the various parties interested in the arms race in one way or another. Many deep friendships exist between procurement and development officials and the leaders of the arms industries. They have bet their futures, often their honor, on each other. Chairmen of powerful Congressional committees usually hold their positions much longer than the principal officers in the executive branch do, and over the years they develop strong feelings of fatherly responsibility for the programs, agencies, and persons that come within their jurisdiction. They often act to promote the programs and causes of these agencies and men without too much regard for their content, and the agency heads and their minions reciprocate with various open and covert demonstrations of admiration and affection.

These political forces are magnified by the gross misapplication of "worst-case analysis," a method of analysis that makes it utterly impossible for both superpowers simultaneously to recognize any given strategic situation as being safe for each of them.

These human failings are ' exaggerated by a widely held myth: that technical experts—generals, scientists, strategic analysts—have some special knowledge making it possible for them, and only them, to arrive at sound political judgments about the arms race. This belief is held not only by much of the general public, but also by many of the experts themselves. And it is made all the more plausible by lavish use of secrecy whenever the debates begin to get tough.

The net result of all this over the years since World War II has been the creation of a defense establishment and an arms industry that are very much bigger than they need to be. The people who inhabit this oversized military-industrial complex in turn form the constituency supporting those elements of the Congress that automatically endorse any weapons development program. Thus a vicious spiral has been created that gives the arms race a "mad momentum" of its own and drives it forward blindly and faster than necessary without regard for, and in spite of, the absurd situations that have been steadily arising from it.

I have not attempted to assess the causes of the strategic-arms race and I have not tried to apportion the blame for its existence. Rather, I have examined many of the separate steps by which it has reached the incredible situation now facing us, and I have found in the majority of those cases that the rate and scale of the individual steps has, in the final analysis, been determined by unilateral actions of the United States.

To be sure, in most cases the taking of each step in the first place has been the almost inevitable result of some combination of preceding steps taken by the Soviets as well as ourselves. But even so, the reaction typically far outran the cause. Accordingly, it is fair to say that the size of our reaction was unilaterally determined by us.

I do not suggest that Einstein and Szilard are culpable for their mistaken assessment of the German A-bomb program, or that those of us on the Von Neumann Committee should be chastised for encouraging and endorsing too many different kinds of big ballistic-missile systems in the mid-fifties, or that the people who promoted all those wild ideas in the wake of Sputnik should be summarily banned from public life. Each of those mistakes and many others like them were made in the context of a totally new situation. Plenty of prudence was, in my view, justified at the time. But the strategic-arms race is now almost a third of a century old. We must learn from these past mistakes that such excessive prudence is itself dangerous and can no longer be justified. Similarly, the frantic concern and zeal rampant in the land after Sputnik that stimulated so many wild ideas can also be explained and excused by the novelty of that situation. We were all surprised by the sudden emergence of the Soviet Union as a first-rate technological power; the reaction Sputnik engendered was nearly universal. But being surprised once ought to be enough; continued over-reactions to a series of lesser surprises cannot be condoned. On the contrary, the public safety demands that they be stopped.

Why has the United States been responsible for the majority of the actions that have set the rate and scale of the arms race? Why have we led the entire world in this mad rush toward the ultimate absurdity?

The reason is not that our leaders have been less sensitive to the dangers of the arms race, it is not that our leaders are less wise, it is not that we are more aggressive or less concerned about the dangers to the rest of mankind. Rather, the reasons are that we are richer and more powerful, that our science and technology are more dynamic, that we generate more ideas of all kinds. For these very reasons, we can and must take the lead in cooling the arms race, in putting the genie back into the bottle, in inducing the rest of the world to move in the direction of arms control, disarmament and sanity.

Just as our unilateral actions were in large part responsible for the current dangerous state of affairs, we must expect that unilateral moves on our part will be necessary if we are ever to get the whole process reversed.

It may be beyond our power to control or eliminate the underlying causes of the arms race by unilateral actions on our part. Our unilateral actions certainly have determined its rate and scale to a very large degree. Very probably our unilateral actions can determine whether we move in the direction of further escalation or in the direction of arms control and, in the long run, nuclear disarmament.

Conventional good sense urges us to keep quiet, to leave these matters to the experts and the technicians. My father, troubled by my repeated trips East to testify against the ABM, asked me, "Why are you fighting City Hall?" His metaphor is sound; the defense establishment is indeed our City Hall, and it can be depended upon to care for its own interests, whether or not these are the interests of the entire nation. If we are to avoid oblivion, if we are to reject the ultimate absurdity, then all of us, not just the current "in" group of experts and technicians, must involve ourselves in creating the policies and making the decisions necessary to do so.

A GLOSSARY OF ACRONYMS

ABM: Anti–ballistic-missile. Any of a number of different systems designed to intercept missile warheads.

AEC: The U. S. Atomic Energy Commission.

AMSA: Advanced manned strategic aircraft. Beginning in the mid-sixties, the designation for the next long-range bomber.

ANP: Aircraft Nuclear Propulsion. A program whose objective was the development of an aircraft powered by nuclear energy.

ARDC: The Air Research and Development Command of the U. S. Air Force.

ARPA: The Advanced Research Projects Agency. A part of the Office of the Secretary of Defense.

A-1, -2, -3: Designations for various versions of the Polaris missile.

BMEWS: Ballistic-missile early-warning system. Huge radars and associated equipment designed to detect a missile attack about 15 minutes before the warheads arrive.

B-17, -29, etc.: Designation for Air Force long-range bombers.

CEP: Circular error probable. Ideally, the radius of a circle within which half of a large number of warheads would fall if all of them were fired at the same center.

DDRE: The Director of Defense Research and Engineering. The official in the Office of the Secretary of Defense charged with the responsibility for all research, development, test and evaluation programs in the Department of Defense.

241

DEW line: Distant early-warning line. A radar system located in the Far North whose purpose is to detect attacking bombers.

FOBS: Fractional orbital bombardment system. A low-flying, long-range missile attack system.

F-104, -108, etc.: Air Force designation for fighter aircraft.

GSETD: General systems engineering and technical direction. A technique for managing very large programs.

ICBM: Intercontinental ballistic missile.

IRBM: Intermediate-range ballistic missile. A missile whose range is typically 1,000–2,000 miles.

IGY: International Geophysical Year: July, 1957, through December, 1958.

JATO: Jet-assisted takeoff. Usually used as the name for small but powerful rockets used to give an extra push at take off to seaplanes, etc.

JCAE: The Joint Committee on Atomic Energy. A joint Senate–House committee having the legislative responsibility for all nuclear-energy programs.

JPL: The Jet Propulsion Laboratory. Operated by the California Institute of Technology for NASA.

K-25: Designation for one of the wartime plants for producing nuclear explosives.

MIRV: Multiple independently targetable reentry vehicles. A system enabling one missile to simultaneously strike more than one target.

MRV: Multiple reentry vehicles. A shotgunlike system for bombarding a target area with more than one warhead.

MOL: Manned Orbiting Laboratory. The designation of a specific Air Force project.

MSR: Missile-site radar. Part of the Safeguard ABM system.

NACA: The National Advisory Committee for Aeronautics. Actually the designation of a former system of government laboratories. It ceased to exist in 1958. See NASA.

NASA: The National Aeronautics and Space Administration. A system of laboratories and other facilities formed in 1958 from NACA plus some other missile-development organizations.

NEPA: Nuclear Energy for the Propulsion of Aircraft. The early name for the project whose goal was nuclear-powered flight.

NORAD: North American Air Defense Command. A joint U. S.–Canada command charged with the air defense of all North America.

PAR: Perimeter acquisition radar. A part of the Safeguard ABM system.

PSAC: The President's Science Advisory Committee.

SAC: The Strategic Air Command. A unit of the U. S. Air Force.

SAGE: Semi-Automatic Ground Environment. A system originally intended to integrate and control the air defense of North America.

SAM: The general designation for surface-to-air missiles, ours or theirs.

SAINT: Satellite interceptor. A system designated to rendezvous with somebody else's noncooperative satellite.

SLBM: Sea- (or submarine)-launched ballistic missile. Polaris and Poseidon.

SLV: Space launch vehicle.

SSBN: Nuclear-powered missile-launching submarine.

SS-9, -11, etc.: Our designation for Soviet ICBMs (SS stands for "surface-to surface").

TFX: A controversial fighter-bomber originally intended for Navy and Air Force use.

U-2: Long-range high-altitude U. S. spy plane.

U235: A nuclear explosive. One of the isotopes of the element uranium.

WDD: The Western Development Division. The early designation of the Air Force unit responsible for the development of missiles and satellites.

X-10: Originally a wartime designation for a laboratory at Oak Ridge, Tennessee.

Y-12: One of the huge plants at Oak Ridge for producing nuclear explosives.

INDEX